AF575159

# HIGH TIMES

RON HAVILAND

# High Times

## *Keeping 'Em Flying*

An Aviation Autobiography
by Arthur R. Kennedy
WITH JO ANN RIDLEY

FITHIAN PRESS
Santa Barbara · 1992

Printed in the United States of America.

Book design and typography by Jim Cook

PHOTO CREDITS

Port of Oakland: 16, 19, 25, 43(a), 48(c), 84(b); Courtesy Harvey Christen: 48 (a, b); Courtesy Mrs. Barbara Cooper: 68; Lockheed Aircraft Corporation: 107, 116; Boeing Aircraft Company: 131; Courtesy Robert Anson: 166; Alverca Aerotek International: 196. All other photographs are from the author's collection.

LIBRARY OF CONGRESS CATALOGING-IN-PUBLICATION DATA
Kennedy, Arthur R., 1913–
High times—keep 'em flying: an aviation autobiography/Arthur R. Kennedy with Jo Ann Ridley.
p. cm.
ISBN 1-56474-001-3
1. Kennedy, Arthur R., 1913– ; 2. Aeronautical engineers—United States—Biography. 3. Aeronautics—History—Sources. I. Ridley, Jo Ann, 1925– . II. Title. III. Title: High times, keeping them flying.
TL540.K43A3 1992 91-24970
629.13'0092—dc20 CIP
[B]

# Table of Contents

These memoirs are dedicated to the aircraft mechanics whose direct and largely unheralded contribution to air safety deserves the lasting gratitude of everyone who flies.

# Foreword

DURING THE COURSE of an active life, our paths sometimes cross those of others who have experienced amazing events, or who have lived in fascinating environments. Occasionally we are even privileged to develop a lasting friendship with such an individual—one whose entire adult life has been flavored with a series of significant events and experiences.

I first met Art Kennedy during the summer of 1969 at the Portuguese aircraft repair facility, *Oficinas Generais Matéria Areonautica*, at Alverca near Lisbon, when I was in charge of aircraft maintenance for the Navy's Sixth Fleet in the Mediterranean. At the time, Art worked for the U.S. Air Force and was overseer of U.S. Government Aircraft and Repair Production at this facility. His professional knowledge as a self-taught aeronautical and industrial engineer was immediately impressive.

At first, however, I could hardly resist the inclination to consider this man a masterful "bullshit artist," to use one of his own favorite expressions. It was difficult to imagine that one person could have had so many unusual and interesting personal experiences, experiences that included a number of famous people. But my apprehension was quickly dispelled when I met Polly, Art's elegant and charming wife of thirty-four years. She had shared his experiences, and I realized then that not even the most engaging prevaricator could have maintained the close relationship these two so obviously enjoyed.

Early in our acquaintance, I suggested that Art should write of his experiences. But it wasn't until ten years later, when he was working as a production engineer at the Naval Plant Representative's office at the Douglas Aircraft Company in Long Beach, that I began a persistent effort to encourage this documentation of a lifetime spanning a good part of the history of aviation. Fortunately for aviation history he has done it, always with the encouragement and support of his attractive and talented second wife, Lidia.

I do not think of this book as a tribute only to the author, but to all of those doggedly persistent aviation pioneers among the ranks of the frequently unrecognized support personnel. They willingly sacrificed so much—including their lives—for the privilege of working on the frontiers of aviation.

I can only hope that Art's labors as he sat at his forty-year-old portable typewriter working to bring you this account, will be rewarded with the knowledge that he has now also made a contribution to the recording of aviation history.

Captain Edmund W. Melvin, USN (Retired)

Pebble Beach, California
July 1991

# Co-author's Acknowledgments

THAT ARTHUR KENNEDY should have settled, quite coincidentally, in the Portuguese village where Sacadura Cabral was born should not surprise those who know him. Aviation notables have floated in and out of his remarkable life with astonishing regularity. Nor, I suppose, should it be cause for wonder that through yet another coincidence, our chance meeting in a Lisbon restaurant, his dream of sharing that remarkable life with others has come to pass.

It has been an adventure. The transcontinental perils of editing a highly personal account, and performing the peripheral research to confirm recall and ensure its accuracy, were compounded initially by my need for a crash course in aviation history and piston engines. And only slightly secondarily by geography. The author lives in Portugal and I live in California. We managed to overcome both disadvantages, which took impressive patience on the author's part, and the expertise, encouragement, and cooperation of countless generous individuals.

Ed Melvin, who started it all, and his wife, Mary Jane, have become valued, supportive friends for whom a mere "thank you" seems hardly enough. Joseph Andrews, former Boeing aeronautical engineer, and his wife, Carol, were the first to read Art Kennedy's original 650-page manuscript and encourage me to undertake its delightful, if occasionally formidable, challenges. Aviation history buff William G. Taylor was of great help, as were Admiral Stuart Hopkins and Lesley Forden, whose first-hand knowledge of the early days at Oakland Municipal

Airport pointed us in fruitful directions. Donald Ellegood, Robert Loomis, and Felix Lowe supplied expert, friendly impetus to the project as well.

Special thanks go to Ken Ellis, editor of Britain's fine historical aviation publication *Flypast Magazine*, to whom we are deeply indebted for vital information in the chapters on the author's wartime experiences in England, information we could not have found elsewhere. And also to Norman Froggatt for his helpful reading of the manuscript with a particularly keen British eye.

Elinor Smith Sullivan, who as a teenager flew her way into the hearts of aviation enthusiasts during the twenties and thirties, offered more encouragement and help than she will ever know. Harvey Christen, of the original Lockheed Company staff and now retired, gave us much appreciated support, thanks to Bill Spaniel of the Lockheed Aeronautical Systems public information office. Others from the colorful Kennedy past who read and confirmed these accounts were Robert Anson, former SALA executive in Costa Rica, and Francisco Quina in Lisbon. Flying friends who supported my conviction that the Kennedy story is indeed unique included Arthur Morse, FAA veteran Lyle Ditzler, John Wingate, Jr., Alan McPherson, and Virginia Trumbull. Novelist Ruth Beebe Hill, who knows what it is to dedicate a whole lifetime to one cherished goal, was an appreciated hand-holder throughout. Special thanks, too, to Admiral Gene Tissot (USN Retired) and Vice Admiral Donald D. Engen (USN Retired) for their invaluable assistance.

We are grateful to the Port of Oakland for access to its treasury of early Oakland Municipal Airport photos and records, the FAA in Oklahoma City for its congenial research, and the San Diego Aerospace Museum, which made the Eddie Cooper Airmail Pioneer collection available. Barbara Cooper lent considerable expertise in providing material about her late husband.

The two people who patiently endured our zeal and determination to see this story in print—our respective spouses, Lidia Kennedy and John Ridley—deserve special gratitude. Finally, to Arthur R. Kennedy himself, thank you for keeping me flying for five fascinating years.

# Prologue

DURING THE EARLY FIFTIES, when I was technical advisor for Avianca in Barranquilla, Colombia, I was invited to Hartford, Connecticut, to accept for that airline an award from Pratt & Whitney for the best engine performance record during the previous year. While I was there, Pratt & Whitney asked me to address a service department symposium, an annual event the company sponsored to keep itself and the airlines abreast of technical developments in the industry.

I was introduced by an old friend, P&W's Robert Bensinger, who began, "The first speaker we all know as a great bullshit artist, but, as many of us here also know, you don't try to prove him wrong, because he always tells the truth. Art's only problem is that he likes to *talk!*"

The room burst into laughter; most of the aviation people there knew me well enough to agree with Bob. But to their surprise—and possible relief—I spoke very briefly and then spent another hour and a half answering questions from an audience composed primarily of men with degrees in aeronautical engineering.

Except for a few extension courses at the University of California, I learned what I know about airplane engines from nearly half a century of working with them, under many circumstances and in many parts of the world. I'll admit to a penchant for regaling friends with accounts of some extraordinary experiences during my aviation career, but after some of those friends suggested that I should write down these stories, that began to seem like a good idea, too. I didn't get around to it, however, until my good friend Ed Melvin pushed so hard that I finally sat down at my forty-year-old Royal portable typewriter and started to pound them out. The recollections unfolded in sharp focus, like a long newsreel, and I became aware that what has happened to me during more than fifty years in aviation is rarely granted to just one man's lifetime. These memoirs, then, are gratefully offered in tribute to those who are seldom given enough credit for their crucial work with aircraft: the mechanics who keep them flying.

The story begins late in the afternoon of the easiest date in history for an aviation buff to remember—the day the world got news of Charles Lindbergh's solo flight across the Atlantic. I was fourteen years old, sauntering out of the YMCA on 19th and Telegraph in Oakland, California, with little on my mind until I heard the newsboys on every corner shouting, "Extree! . . . Extree! . . . First successful transatlantic flight . . . Lindbergh crosses the ocean alone!"

It was not the first successful transatlantic flight, of course. Lindbergh was the first to do it alone nonstop, but in the excitement on May 21, 1927, few recalled that the U.S. Navy, the British rigid airship R-34, and pilots J.W. Alcock and A. Whitten Brown had done it in 1919, or that two Portuguese flyers, Sacadura Cabral and Gago Coutinho, had crossed the South Atlantic by air in 1922.

I raced down the street, bought a newspaper with the only nickel I had, and sat down to read it. Totally absorbed in the front page account of Lindbergh's feat, I suddenly realized that it was getting dark, and the nickel I'd paid for the paper was my carfare home. The only thing I remember about the forty-block walk to our house at 60th and Shattuck is that my head was in the clouds as I went over in my mind every detail of the flight and fantasized about what it must be like to fly in Lindy's "great silver bird." I had caught the aviation bug of the twenties and there would be no cure for it.

From that moment on I collected anything I could find about aviation. In my family, which didn't have very much money, if you wanted something, you worked for it. I cut the neighbors' lawns for ten cents each to earn money to buy *Western Flying*. Then I carefully snipped out the picture of airplanes and made a scrapbook of everything that was flying. I still have it—a crisp and yellowed sixty-year-old reminder of the astounding variety of aircraft aloft in 1927.

As a lot of kids were doing then, a boy in our neighborhood built a model of Lindbergh's NX-211. I thought it was horrible, and ragged him shamelessly about how lousy it was until finally he gave it to me with the parting shot that I only wanted it because I couldn't make one as good. To a cocky kid like me, that was an irresistible challenge.

My father was a carpenter; he allowed me to use his good tools as long as I kept them clean and sharp, which he carefully taught me how to do. I took the model apart, collected dimensional drawings of the NX-211, and set about rebuilding it.

I was right. It was badly out of proportion, so I decided to make a better one. I worked on it every spare moment, tearing apart, rebuilding, and learning the hard way that mistakes can be valuable if you let them teach you something. Such determined model-building severely tested my family's patience, especially when I glued balsa wood to the dining room table; for that dereliction I ate off the mantel for a week. My father offered no help as I struggled, but he was watching closely.

Finally I finished my own *Spirit of St. Louis*. I thought it was beautiful, exactly like the real one. Hanging from the light fixture over my bed, it was the first and last thing I saw every day.

When I showed my plane to my manual training teacher, he suggested that I enter it in a model airplane contest at the Oakland Auditorium. This I confidently did, certain I would take first place. But, as I cruised around the auditorium looking at the other entries, I was brought up short by a beautiful Boeing 40B4 biplane mounted on an elaborate pedestal. Even the louvers on the cowling worked! It had been made by one of my classmates at University High, a boy named Gordon Lamb. As I anxiously stared at his masterpiece, he strolled up and asked what I was doing there. "Oh, nothing," I lied, "just looking around." Gordon was only too happy to show me every exquisite detail of the model, how all the controls actually worked, even to the landing gear bungees. I knew he had put twice the time and effort into it that I put into the NX-211, and I knew it would win the $50 first prize, which it did. A Monocoupe model took second, and I went home with the $5 third prize.

Properly humbled, I vowed to make no more models. The *Spirit of St. Louis* spent the rest of her life on top of our upright piano. My mother, at least, was very proud of it.

That vow lasted only until I started visiting the Oakland Municipal Airport in 1928 and began making small, six-inch models of the airplanes I saw there. My collection eventually included a Stearman C3-B, a Waco 9, a Waco taperwing, an Eaglerock long and short wing, three Travel Airs with the OX-5, Hisso "E," Comet engines, a Velie-powered Monocoupe, a Monoprep, a J-5 Pitcairn, an OX-5 Bird, a Fairchild Razorback, and the Curtiss Robin later used by "Wrong Way" Corrigan.

Early in 1929 my occasional visits to the airport became regular weekend excursions that soon were the focal point of my teenage life. Carfare cost ten cents round trip, so I had to hustle. I sold the *Saturday Evening Post* and delivered the *Oakland Tribune*, and before long I won a pair of Union Hardware roller skates for promptness and new sales. The skates got me through the two jobs faster than before, so I could spend even more time at the airport.

My next goal was to earn enough to buy an airplane ride, which Metro Air Service advertised at $5 for two people on Sundays. I promoted some more lawn-mowing customers and finally accumulated $2.50, my heart set on flying with the famous stunt pilot Franklin Rose in Metro's hot J-5 Stearman C3-B, which sported a beautiful green fuselage and white wings with black struts.

Proudly showing the ride salesman my sweaty handful of coins, I announced "I want an airplane ride and I have the $2.50!" He said, "But, sonny, rides are two for $5 or one for $3." I was stunned. After an eternal pause, the salesman said, "I'll tell you what; I'll waive my commission and go with you for the $2.50." I started breathing again and we walked out to the Stearman. He took Rose aside and talked with him for a minute, but Rose hardly glanced at me as we climbed aboard. It never occurred to me to wonder why the salesman strapped me in extra tight before we took off.

I'll never forget that ride. Rose made the plane do everything a stunt plane could do, a lot of it either vertical or upside down, with me hanging against the cockpit belt in dizzy ecstasy.

I'm sure they were trying to make me airsick, or at least scare me to death. But they couldn't do it. The only thing I knew, as we landed, was that I was going to spend the rest of my life around airplanes. And that's exactly what I did.

# HIGH TIMES

*Keeping 'Em Flying*

*Oakland Municipal Airport, 1930. Hangar #3, lower left, housed Metro Air Service and Boeing Air Transport. Hangar #2 was home base for Pacific Aeromotive's Oakland operation and local and transient operators. Airport restaurant where author had his "first solo flight" breakfast is in center surrounded by crowd. Western Airlines housed Fokker F-VIIs in Hangar #1 adjacent to airport administration building and, at far upper right, nation's first airport inn. Crowd on flight line surrounds Charles Kingsford Smith's Fokker V-VIIab-3m "Southern Cross." To left of Fokker are two Stinson Reliants, and next to them Metro's C3-B Stearmans, including the "Green Hornet."*

CHAPTER 1

# The Metro Gang

IN 1929 I BEGAN to spend my summer vacations seriously hanging around the Metro Air Service bunch at hangar #3. In those days the Oakland Municipal Airport was located immediately north of the present major facility on Bay Farm Island south of Alameda. Formerly it had been called "Bay Farm Island Airport." Its original 800 acres of flatland constituted a network of muddy sloughs on the western edge of Oakland, bounded by South San Francisco across the Bay to the west and San Leandro Bay and Alameda Island on the north. Oakland had first looked to the skies on October 12, 1912, when one Weldon B. Cooke took to the air in a little bird that looked somewhat like today's ultralight aircraft.

Obsessed by my growing passion for airplanes, I was barely tolerating school, and history meant nothing to me. So I was neither aware of nor even interested in the fact that after only two years of operation, Oakland's airport had become the West Coast's leading aviation facility. It had been built in June, 1927, when a farsighted Port of Oakland met the Army Air Service's challenge to prepare, within two weeks, the 7020-foot runway from which Lieutenants Les Maitland and Al Hegenberger took off for the first Pacific crossing by air from San Francisco to Honolulu. Another, less fortunate, Army attempt in July and in August the Dole race to Hawaii put Oakland on the aviation map—not only because of those more or less spectacular accomplishments but because of the area's nearly perfect flying conditions. Relatively free of hazards (the Oakland hills are far to the northeast), it was unusually safe. Visibility was always good, with a ceiling that seldom dropped below 600 feet. Smartly seizing on the momentum of events, the Port of Oakland turned the marshy little airport into a permanent development, with elaborate drainage systems to control the sloughs and high tides flowing in from the bay.

Only two months after the transatlantic flight that had exploded into my excited teenage purview, Charles Lindbergh came to Oakland to dedicate the airfield.

"You have here one of the finest airports I have seen," he told the crowd. "Oakland is setting an example to the cities of the country." I knew he was coming and longed to go out to see him; but, as usual, I couldn't scrape up the carfare to get to the airport.

Even as my little world was centered on the relatively small Metro Air Service operation there, Oakland was, in fact, operating the largest commercial airport in the West, home to several airlines and fixed base operations, the Department of Commerce Aeronautics Branch for the Western States, and a Navy aviation training base. Aviation technology was hurtling into the 1930s with Oakland on the leading edge. There, in 1928, pilots could taxi up to the only compass swinging table in the United States; in 1929 the government established there the first airways weather reporting system in the country; and the airport's huge night-landing beacon was the talk of pilots everywhere. Oakland was also the Western terminus for the airmail system. Eddie Rickenbacker flew in the first load of transcontinental mail. The ever-ambitious Port dug a channel to the edge of the airport and constructed a float where a speedboat picked up the mail and transported it eleven miles across the Bay to San Francisco. Some aviation publications even favorably compared Oakland with the famous Berlin-Tempelhof field in Germany.

The man supervising this impressive operation in the late twenties was the affable and efficient Guy "Pop" Turner, a former Navy chief who was one of aviation's most popular administrators. Pop was a good friend to me at a crucial time in my young life.

The callow innocence I brought to this heady aviation milieu must have been a source of considerable amusement to the hardbitten folks

*Guy "Pop" Turner in trademark puttees (left) confers with Department of Commerce official, Oakland Municipal Airport, 1927.*

at Metro. I was a skinny sixteen-year-old, small for my age, wet behind the ears, crazy in love with airplanes, and already possessed of a smart mouth.

The company was named for its two owners, Sammy Metzger and Franklin Rose. Metzger, about whom I knew little, ran the financial part of the operation, controlling the purse strings none too loosely. Rose, a former Varney Air Lines mail pilot and then still a famous barnstormer, ran the aviation part of the business. His distinguished career, which began in the early twenties, later took him to Southern California and then to Europe. He served as commanding general of the 325th Air Division of the Air Force Reserve headquartered at Hamilton Field north of San Francisco, and well into World War II also served as a general in MATS, which ran military air transportation operations out of Bay Area headquarters.

Metzger and Rose employed a particularly memorable mechanic named Phil Hungerford, best known around the field as "Foulmouth Phil." The talk at Hangar #3 was usually about either airplanes or pussy. It took me a while to understand what pussy was, but Phil was a dedicated instructor in both subjects. When it became obvious that I wasn't going to go away, Frank finally put me to work helping assemble and rig the Stearman airplanes that arrived at the Metro dealership in big boxes. He was an exacting teacher; to this day I have a fetish about tightening cotter pins. Before long they also talked me into washing airplanes, for which Frank offered either minimum pay or a few minutes of flying time. I was so anxious to get into the air that there wasn't much choice. Other pilots also began to offer stick time in exchange for keeping their airplanes clean. That's how I learned to fly. To earn carfare to this aeronautical heaven, I joined the crew that sold airplane ride tickets for Frank's Sunday air shows.

It was an exciting time. Huge crowds always showed up when Franklin Rose advertised a show because in this heyday of air shows, Frank's were among the best. Barnstormers were the visible aspect of civil aviation for the few who saw them in the early twenties; but after the Lindbergh flight in 1927, aviation grabbed the public's imagination in earnest and whole families would come to the Oakland airport, where Pop Turner set aside a picnic area so they could make a day of it. Airshows gave the public an inexpensive thrill in a circus-like atmosphere, especially during the Depression when few people had money to spend on entertainment.

Regulars at the Oakland shows included well-known flyers like "Wee Willie" Willingham, whose repeated loop-the-loops and slow barrel rolls in his cream-colored Waco 9 powered with an OX-5 engine were a wonder to behold. Major Livingston Irving, of the Army Reserve Squadron, made "death defying" parachute jumps that always elicited gasps from the crowd; Gene Legault, billed as "The Crazy Frenchman," in his Hisso "E" speedwing Travel Air performed speed runs about twenty feet off the ground close to the spectators, pulling up into a beautiful chandelle and finishing with a slow roll out.

I was always glad to hear that Gene was entering a show. Because he had the habit of indulging in a few brandies before he flew, he tended to relax as soon as he felt the ground after landing. In a slight cross-wind this would frequently result in a ground loop, usually crushing at least three ribs on the left wing aft of the spar. Each time this happened I got ten dollars for repairing the ribs and recovering and painting the wing tip, a skill I had learned well from Frank Rose.

Airplane rides for the public were a big part of the show, so business always picked up when Ben Filmore brought in his series 6000 Travel Air. He would load up the six-passenger high-wing monoplane with a bunch of kids and take them up for free rides to prove that aviation really was safe. Once Ben had landed with the kids intact, their folks would stand in line to buy a ride with him. It seems analogous to the court taster surviving a meal before the king ate, but we sold a lot of rides thanks to Filmore.

Today, more than sixty years later, I realize what a privilege it was to watch Frank Rose stage those shows. They were a veritable circus aloft complete with rides, stunts, and races; but in my star-glazed teenage eyes, the most exciting part was the grand finale, when Frank sponsored a three-pylon free-for-all race. Frank flew his famous "Green Hornet" (the Stearman I'd had my first ride in), and always beat the faster planes with his superior flying and tight vertical turns close to the ground.

One of the few times Frank felt threatened was when a really fast Pitcairn J-5 showed up with a new engine cowling just approved by the National Advisory Commission for Aeronautics. Despite the Pitcairn's improved aerodynamics, however, Frank still managed to take first place. There's no doubt that Franklin Rose was one of the foremost pilots of his day.

Frank's airshows came to be considerably enlivened by the first airplane I ever saw that could exceed 150 miles an hour. It was a C4E Stearman, a large biplane powered by the new 300 J-6-9 Wright engine, and it had a big, comfortable cockpit. Jonathon Hale, of the movies, owned it and took to flying up from his Pebble Beach home every weekend to let Frank borrow it for the Sunday races. Inevitably, Frank would be first across the line and would finish with his most spectacular stunts, finally pulling a high loop after diving almost to the ground. It was a great crowd-pleaser for spectators more accustomed to watching less powerful airplanes lose two to three thousand feet after each stunt, then waiting for them to climb back to altitude for the next one. We couldn't sell tickets fast enough to keep up with the long lines of people eager to go up with Frank after they'd seen him fly Hale's Stearman.

The Oakland shows attracted flyers from all over Northern California. One Sunday the Orange brothers, who owned an airport near Bakersfield, came in with a spanking-new dark red cabin Cessna, powered with a J-6-9 like Hale's. She was a clean bird with a full cantilever wing and no external struts. It even *looked* fast, and we knew Frank might be in trouble. However, when they said they would not enter the stunting contest because the bird was not maneuverable enough, Frank figured that in a race he could beat them on the turns and continue to win the free-for-all.

In those days, racing planes took off race-horse style, lined up wing to wing with engines idling until the flag dropped to send them roaring out of the gate. The trick was to be first around the first pylon. There were eight planes that day, and right away that damn Cessna was way ahead of everyone! Our hearts dropped, but at the first turn the Cessna had to take it high and wide, and as it leveled off Frank took the lead, making his typical tight vertical turns close to the ground. This went on for the whole race. At the end they called it a tie and we took only half the prize money.

A revenge race was scheduled, and for a solid month I watched Frank practice turns at altitude, trying to find out the maximum he could pull without blacking out, and whether the bird would fall out of a high-speed vertical turn. On race day the Orange brothers' Cessna flew in from Bakersfield with a new high-gloss paint job, well waxed down. We had waxed our bird, too, picking up almost five miles an hour. Frank was not concerned. He knew the competition had been too busy with charter work and the paint job to do much practicing. A friend of his had managed to buy a little time in the red Cessna and told Frank that the turns he'd seen in Oakland were the maximum she would do. Frank thought they would be more cautious on the turns, and he was right. Before the tenth lap he had picked up so much lead that he breezed across the finish line far ahead of the Cessna.

Hoping to recoup their pride, the Orange brothers invited us all, ticket sellers and mechanics included, to their Orange airport in Bakersfield for an important meet with big money prizes. They also invited what we liked to call the "Hollywood glamour boy" stunt pilots. Paul Mantz, Frank Clarke, Leo Nomis, and Frank Tallman were among those who showed up, and even Frank Rose acknowledged there would be some dangerous flying competition.

That meet was my initiation into what I regarded as the aviation big time, an exciting first opportunity to see these famous flyers in action. Still a teenager but now a full-fledged member of the Oakland airport gang, I flew down to Bakersfield with them in a contingent of twenty planes and slept that night in the cockpit of the C-4E under blankets furnished by Frank's wife, Mildred Rose.

Mildred, a tiny but great lady, not only was a hell of a flyer herself, but she was my surrogate mother during the years I hung out at the Oakland airport. Mildred and Frank lived in the Piedmont enclave of Oakland and had a young son of their own. Occasionally I'd stay with Buddy while his folks were flying, and I remember once extricating him from a ceiling girder of the Metro hangar following a climbing escapade. Even then, Frank Jr. was as cool as his father, and later was to distinguish himself as a fighter pilot in World War II, where he was lost. Devoted as the Roses were to their son, Mildred's heart was big enough for me, too, and I shall forever love her for putting up with my cocky adolescence.

Saturday night before the meet in Bakersfield, the hosts threw a big party for us in one of the hangars. About midnight we heard a plane and went out to see if some drunk had decided to go flying. Frank Clarke, who had not been drinking with the others, was taking off in his souped-up speedwing Travel Air with clipped wings. Everyone went back to the party, but Clarke broke it up again by flying low and slow over the hangar and dumping a sack of ball bearings on the metal roof. When the crowd rushed outside to see what was going on, he jettisoned a load of garbage out of the cockpit and made a direct hit on a couple of dozen upturned faces. They were still hosing themselves off when Frank landed, laughing like hell. The ball bearing trick was a Clarke trademark I witnessed more than once.

The next morning, Frank Rose made an early reconnaissance of the race course and dejectedly reported to the Oakland gang that the Orange brothers had placed the race pylons at three times the distance he was used to. Even with bad turns, their Cessna would have the distance and time to overtake the competition. The Hollywood flyers, who hadn't known about the red Cessna until they got to Bakersfield, were beginning to worry, too. A lot of prize money was at stake.

During the stunting contests that traditionally preceded the big race, our Livingston Irving easily won the spot parachute jump, and Hollywood's Leo Nomis won the handkerchief pick-up competition, the only pilot who actually picked up the handkerchief from the ground, flying a Great Lakes with swept-back wings and powered with a Menasco Pirate engine. Then came the aerobatics. Frank Rose drew the short straw and went up first, knowing he had to be perfect from the start. And he was!

At take-off Frank held the bird on the ground until the very end of the field, pulled up sharp and over on his back, came back down the field, and then made the finest Immelman roll I've ever seen executed, to this day. Then he pulled up to a thousand feet, performed an exceptionally smooth series of stunts, and finished off with a perfect hesitation roll.

I don't think Frank had ever done that stunt before and nobody could touch him. But Frank Clarke had to try. He must have had a remarkable memory, because he copied Rose's stunt exactly, except that in the hesitation roll he hesitated inverted, and possibly because of the Travel Air's clipped wings the bird fell out and into a spin. Excellent pilot that he was, Clarke managed to pull out a few feet from disaster and took second place to our Frank's first.

Finally it was time for the event everyone was waiting for. But just as the big race was announced and engines rumbled into action, we saw a great commotion around the Orange brothers' red Cessna and rushed over to see what was going on. The engine had been switched off. The pilot sat hunched in the cockpit, speechless with anger. He was not going to fly. Apparently one of the ground crew had noticed something peculiar about the airplane as the pilot started the engine; looking closer, he discovered that someone had used a knife to cut the entire belly out of the fabric-covered ship.

Frank Rose was standing next to Frank Clarke in the crowd surrounding the Cessna. "The dirty bastard that did that should have his balls cut off," he said. "I refuse to enter a race that SOB is afraid to fly!" "That goes double for me," said Frank Clarke, and so many other pilots dropped out that the committee had to cancel the race. Although there was a lot of talk about one of the Hollywood stunt men, they never really knew who did it. It left a sour taste in everyone's mouth, and I heard talk that it would be a long time before outsiders were invited to privately sponsored airshows again.

The Metro gang renewed its acquaintance with the Hollywood flyers when they came to Oakland to shoot post-release dogfight footage for the great Howard Hughes picture *Hell's Angels*. In those smogless days, Los Angeles skies were too clear for cloud effects.

*Three decades after: West Coast aviation greats at 1961 dedication of new Oakland International Airport facilities. Seated (left to right): Albert Hegenberger, Ernie Smith, Livingston Irving. Standing: James Warner and Paul Mantz.*

Oakland, however, had cumulus clouds in abundance, which gave the otherwise vast sky the needed dimensional effect on film. Hughes's crew brought some real Fokker D-7s and a beautifully restored SE-5, and during the shooting there was great excitement when Roscoe Turner flew in with his Sikorsky S-29 remodeled to look like a German Gotha.

Elmer Dyer, one of the famous cameramen of his day, was to use our C-3B J-5 Stearman for the camera ship. We modified the front cockpit for the instruments and controls, then enlarged the rear cockpit to mount the camera on a Lewis gun gimbal. Either Frank or his brother, Clarence ("Nip") Rose, flew this camera plane. Frank Clarke, Paul Mantz, and Leo Nomis were flying the other planes, along with a Northern California contingent of pilots from Mills Field—now the San Francisco International Airport—among them Bob Six, Jimmy Angel, and Captain Bill Royle. Like a number of people involved in the early days of Northern California aviation, I particularly remem ber their crackerjack mechanic named Eddie Shine, who could fix anything.

As is normal in movie making, the crew had to kill a lot of time waiting to shoot. Pilots mostly sat in front of the hangar drinking and playing cards, and occasionally Frank Clarke livened things up by dumping ball bearings on the hangar roof. But there was always a fast scramble to shoot the dogfight sequences when the right cloud formation appeared, and everything became very serious. In one memorable scene the pilot, played by Leo Nomis, was supposed to forget to fasten his safety belt and fall out of the cockpit during a maneuver, landing on top of the fuselage just in front of the vertical fin. The falling out part was a studio shot. The location crew had to film him desperately trying to get back into the cockpit while still in the air.

For this sequence, we covered the front cockpit of Gene Legault's Travel Air and cut a window in each side so the pilot could see out. Then we cut handholds in the side of the fuselage where Leo could hang on before creeping back to the pit.

Since the studio paid well for damage occurring during shooting, and Gene needed a recover job, he figured this was a good time to get it. He told Leo to dig his heels into the side of the fuselage so it would come back badly torn. They took off, Leo sitting on the fuselage and Nip following in the Stearman. Within range of some nice afternoon clouds, Nip closed up and Elmer Dyer started grinding.

Disgracefully overacting—after all he was a pilot, not an actor—Leo managed to make his way into the cockpit of the Travel Air. Back on the ground again, Elmer said, "Damn it, Leo, you're sure as hell no actor. This isn't a Keystone Cop comedy! You're supposed to be trying to save your life. Next time, just crawl!"

About then, Gene strolled up. "Look what that SOB did to the side of my fuselage!" he said in feigned surprise. The director ordered me to get some linen and dope and patch it quick so they could get back to shooting. But Gene didn't want a patch, he wanted the fuselage recovered. He disappeared for a minute, and when he came back I saw him put a pair of rowled spurs on Leo's boots. They went up for the retake and landed with the side of the fuselage torn to ribbons. The spurs were nowhere to be seen.

Gene got his recover job, and I made $75 doing it. It seemed like a fortune. I was just getting interested in girls, so I took my date to the best restaurant in Oakland and a show. I was a big shot kid!

Or so I thought. One day Nip Rose got sick and couldn't fly the camera plane. They were going for a close-up of Frank Clarke as Lt. Von Bruen, handsome and very authentic in his German flying helmet, goggles, and the requisite thin mustache, in the cockpit of a Fokker. Knowing I could use the money, they let me take Nip's place.

After explicit instructions from Elmer, I took off, found the clouds he wanted to shoot, and Frank hugged them close while I came in at about thirty degrees from in front and eased up to him.

Hoping to impress the famous cameraman, I kept coming in until I was only inches away from the Fokker. Then we hit some unexpected turbulence and I had a hell of a time keeping away from Frank, who was frantically waving me off. Elmer signaled that he had enough and we went back to the field. When I landed, the director walked up and asked if the take was good. Elmer said that it was, but he wasn't about to go up with the crazy kid again!

Frank Clarke really chewed me out. "What were you trying to do, kill us?" he asked.

"Hell, Frank, we weren't that close, and anyway I had control when we hit the turbulence."

"The hell you did! Look at your wing." I did, and nearly fainted. A long red mark was sliced across the tip of it, as if my carelessness had drawn blood.

After several weeks of shooting, the glamour boys went back to Hollywood and life at the Oakland airport returned to what passed for normalcy in that crazy era.

The Hollywood "invasion" and subsequent events left me with a lot to think about. Following my escapade scraping the paint off the Fokker with the camera plane, I was never asked to fly again during the *Hell's Angels* shoot in Oakland. At sixteen I had learned an important lesson about flying. Overconfidence is a killer. So is showing off.

I redeemed myself in the movie flying business when I moved to Southern California a few years later, a little older and much wiser. Mantz, who was not particularly popular with the Associated Motion Picture pilots because he didn't immediately join their union, for a long time had a corner on the movie stunt flying business. I did some movie work for Paul, who hired me several times either to fly or work on his airplanes, and later involved me in Amelia Earhart's preparations for her round-the-world flight. I was just one of the many aircraft technicians Paul worked with over the years, but I treasure the letter of reference he wrote for me in 1938: "He has unusual qualifications of being not only an excellent airplane mechanic, but one of the finest engine men I have had the pleasure of knowing." Coming from one of the finest pilots I ever had the pleasure of knowing, it was awesomely high praise. Praise, however, that came only after I had literally and figuratively earned my wings the hard way.

## CHAPTER 2

# Airborne

JUDGING BY THE QUALITY of instruction he provided, Frank Rose must have concluded that I was really serious about airplanes and before long offered to let me work on engines with him and Phil. The idea, they said, was to try to make an aircraft mechanic out of me. According to historical files at the Port of Oakland, in 1929 aircraft mechanics there were called "mechanicians" and earned about $80 a month.

I didn't care what I was called, and there would be no pay, of course. But each time we finished working on a Comet Stearman Frank would give me a little dual time in it; if I was really lucky he'd even ease me through a landing. As we assembled and rigged the new planes, he patiently showed me how to start and properly run up the engine. When they were sure I had learned that, he and Phil next taught me how to perform a twenty-hour check. I couldn't have had better teachers; they were taskmasters, but patient and detailed in their instruction. Their insistence that I do everything the right way stayed with me for the rest of my life.

By comparison, today's piston engine mechanics have it pretty easy. The engines of my day didn't have overhead lubrication, so you had to remove all the rocket box covers, then the adjusting screw and push rods. These were thoroughly cleaned, dipped into heavy grease, and reinstalled. Then the valve clearance had to be reset, and the rocker box covers reinstalled and secured with brass safety wire. Frank would raise holy hell with me if the wire wasn't twisted tightly and neatly. I learned to pull, clean, and reinstall the oil filter and then check the magnetos. The points had to be filed, cleaned, set, and synchronized. Then I cleaned the fuel filter, oiled the controls, and checked them for full range movement. The final task was to run up the engine and replace the cowl.

It was a lot to learn, but I thrived on it. One day Frank told me I was doing great and bought me some overalls, the smallest pair he could find. I was so little for my age that the overalls had to be rolled up at the sleeves and pant legs. The crotch fell almost to my knees. In my hip pocket I always carried a couple of wooden blocks I had made from a 2×4 with straps to attach to my shoes so I could reach the rudder pedals when I flew. You never knew when there would be a chance to go up with someone. I must have been a pretty comical figure. Around the airport I was known simply as "The Kid."

Life was perfect except for one thing. Although I was getting good dual time in the air with different flyers whose airplanes I helped service, nobody ever offered me a chance to solo. Maybe it was because I was so small, or they thought I was too young. Whatever the reason, it seemed to me that it was a dream that wasn't going to come true.

One of my flight instructors was a fellow named Bob Jellison. Early one Sunday morning Bob was expecting a student and asked me to gas up his Monoprep. She was a pretty little two-place tandem parasol open aircraft with a five-cylinder Velie radial engine. Pushing her out of the hangar was no trouble, but it was a long push to the gas pit way down the field, so I decided to taxi.

She responded well. What wind there was came right on the nose. It felt so good that I opened it up a bit. That was even better. Then I opened her a little more. The controls felt just like they did when I'd had dual time with Bob. For a little more thrill, I lifted the tail a bit. I looked around. There wasn't a soul in sight. What the hell! A little more throttle and we were airborne.

The dream was coming true, but it quickly turned into a nightmare. I was alone in the air for the first time in my life, nobody along to tell me what to do. As Bob had taught me, I carefully eased her up to about 500 feet over the golf course just north of the airport and confidently made the first turn. Then the awful truth hit. How was I going to get down? Bob had called my last landing an accident looking for a place to happen, and I began to imagine every possible punishment if I damaged this pretty airplane. Maybe they would even banish me from the airfield, the most terrible punishment of all.

I was shaking as I made a gentle turn into the downwind leg, afraid even to look out to the Oakland hills or San Francisco Bay to the west. Down on the field, however, I could see the windsock up and steady. That, at least, was encouraging. The bad landing last time had been in gusty conditions.

I finally got ahold of myself and realized I had to concentrate on everything I had been taught. Hardly breathing, I came into the base leg. One more turn and we were lined up with the field. Back on the throttle . . . we're on final glide path . . . about fifty feet over the highway . . . time to bring up the nose and slow down.

There was no need to watch the airspeed indicator. Flying in an open cockpit bird without goggles, I'd been taught to judge speed by the feel of the slipstream on my cheeks. Sluggishness in the controls would warn of an approaching stall. I kept easing back and bringing the nose up a little more. The wheels touched. We weren't in a three-point position so I pushed the stick forward and held the wheels on the ground. Whew! No bounce. The tail dropped slowly to the ground and we stopped. I'd done it!

I taxied to the gas pit, terrified to see a reception committee consisting of Bob Jellison and his student, Frank, Mildred, Nip Rose, and even worse, Pop Turner and the airport cop. No doubt about it, they were going to put me in jail! I was scared shitless.

The long-legged owner was first to reach the plane as I shut off the engine. Bob took one look and hollered, "Holy cow! It's the damned Kid!" I climbed out to face Frank, who asked a question I'll never forget. "Was this your first solo?" I nodded. Then Mildred pushed her way through the circle and came defensively to my side.

"You guys should be proud! The Kid just made a perfect wheel landing that Bob said was impossible with this plane. Now you forget what you had in your minds before we saw that, and I'm going to take him to the restaurant and buy him a big plate of ham and eggs!"

"Good idea!" said Pop Turner. "You're all invited to breakfast on me to celebrate The Kid's first solo."

It was too much to handle; I burst into tears. Mildred put her arms around me and I told her how scared I had been. "It's okay," she said. "If you hadn't been afraid you might have wiped out the plane and yourself. Sometimes it helps to be scared. Just don't ever get too cocky." Mildred knew me well enough to realize I'd probably be fighting that battle most of my life. I was a brassy kid, pretty confident, and tended to mouth off when I shouldn't. Sometimes it served me well; other times it just got me into trouble.

One time I did know enough to keep my mouth shut, however. I had always wondered what it felt like to fly in a stunt plane, so, during a Sunday air show, I sneaked into the front cockpit of Wee Willie's Waco, strapping in and hunching down so he couldn't see me. Willie strode out, got in without looking at the front pit, started her up and took off. He climbed to about 5000 feet and began his act. I could hardly keep myself from looking out while Willie pasted that Waco all over the sky. He was such a good pilot that the flight felt smooth as silk. I couldn't fasten the seat belt tightly because I was so slouched down, but only once did it come tight. Now I knew. Flying in a stunt plane was as exhilarating as I thought it would be. I wanted to whoop with joy, but of course I couldn't. Back on the ground I stayed out of sight until Willie was whisked off for a drink with friends.

*Teenage author flew the mail to San Jose in a Boeing 40-B-2 late in 1929.*

But he complained that the bird acted strangely and for several days had every mechanic on the field trying to find out why. I finally admitted to Frank Rose what I had done because I wanted to know what effect my being along had on the Waco. I expected a real chewing out, but he only explained how the extra weight could have had serious consequences, and laughed about Willie's fruitless efforts to locate a nonexistent problem.

Early in my training period, Frank nearly bought the farm himself with the Stearman during one of the last races he ever flew. He had just come in first, and as usual made a spectacular pull-up to a vertical position. At this point, with hardly any airspeed, the engine froze. He wheeled over and we were sure he was going to spin, but thanks to the Stearman's controllability he managed to prevent it and pulled out in time to make a cross wind dead stick landing. He came out of the cockpit pretty shaken and said it was the closest he had ever come to spinning in.

This near-disaster provided my first experience opening an engine when Frank instructed Phil Hungerford to find out why the engine froze, and Phil asked me to help him. The engine was a Wright J-6-9 with a supercharge-blower. We couldn't even turn the prop. During disassembly Phil minutely examined every piece of the engine and explained to me what he found. Everything in the power section was scored and burned, but we couldn't find a reason for the engine freezing up. Then we took apart the blower section and discovered that a seal ring had loosened, turned, and sealed off the oil passage from the blower section to the power section, causing the failure. Since the engine had only eighty hours on it, Wright sent a replacement. And The Kid was beginning to feel like a real mechanic.

Hard work sessions like that were interspersed with occasional barnstorming trips, still a big part of aviation life in the late twenties. The Oakland bunch would go as a group, often making arrangements with a farmer to use his field and advertise that they were coming out to put on an air show. At the more isolated fields, they would charge admission and split the take with the farmer.

One Sacramento Valley farmer near Gridley was willing to exchange the use of his field for "a good airyplane ride." We were amazed at the size of the crowd that showed up, although Frank, Mildred, and I arrived too late to sell many rides that first day. But we weren't too late for the customary Saturday night partying in town. Concerned about leaving fifteen planes unguarded, they hired an old duffer with an antique shotgun to keep watch. I had to stay with him, because they were going to dinner at a saloon, and I was still too young to get into places like that. The old boy wouldn't have let them take me, anyway. He was very religious and spent all night telling me how the devil talked people into drinking and carousing. He also had heard me talk, and delivered a hard lecture about swearing. He was right, but it didn't do a lot of good. I'd been cleaning airplanes all day and was so tired and hungry that I finally stopped listening to his rantings, except that I did hear him warn me against women, which didn't do much good, either. I was still an innocent teenage virgin.

Just when I thought I was going to die from starvation, we saw automobile lights coming out to the field, and the ever-thoughtful Mildred Rose arrived in a large touring car with two big boxes of food and some heavy blankets. I ate well, then spent a comfortable night under the blankets in the cockpit of the Stearman. We were up at sunrise to get ready for the crowd that came early to see the excitement at our makeshift airport. I sold a lot of ride tickets, and about lunchtime a truck showed up with a wood-fired stove, from which a couple of pretty girls—one of whom I later saw in the movies as actress Donna Reed—did a brisk business selling hot dogs, hamburgers, popcorn, and pop. It was a big day in that little northern California community.

Then it was show time. First came the standard acrobatic displays, and then, at long last, the pylon race everyone had come to see. The pilots were especially intent, having collected more than $300 in prize money from local businessmen at the previous night's party in town. The airplanes provided keen competition: two J-5 Stearmans, two J-5 Travel Airs, one Hisso "E" speedwing Travel Air, a taper wing Waco 10 J-5, and a J-5 Pitcairn.

Frank always won these competitions because of his skill in making the lowest and tightest turns and picking up more lead at every pylon. On this particular Sunday he drew the least likely position to make the first pylon ahead of the others.

Two other pilots, who didn't much like Frank, decided to keep him from passing at the pylons. Frank soon realized they were crowding him, so he started going higher and wider, forcing them up with him.

Finally he got them high, approached the pylon in a vertical position, and when they began to crowd him he dove for the deck, went under them, and passed everyone. But it cost him first place. When he taxied in I went out to meet him. "That was close!' he said. "Go take a look at my left wing, Kid, and see if there's any damage." I looked carefully but found no damage except for the wing tip stained where it cut through the wheat field.

Frank was furious and told the two flyers that if they were real pilots they'd accept his challenge to an individual race, but if they were too scared to take him on alone he'd challenge them to a three plane race with their aircraft as prizes. They accused Frank of bluffing, but backed off and apparently took seriously Frank's warning never to share the same skies with him again. After that they never showed up where Frank was flying.

Spending time at the Oakland airport gave me an opportunity to watch the Navy in action there, especially after they got their first Curtiss dive bombers. As their flying techniques improved, the Navy pilots began to fly and even land in tight formations. It was quite a thrill to watch these new maneuvers. One day, when they were at about 3000 feet, five of them wheeled over into a vertical wide open dive. Four planes pulled out over the water at the edge of the airport, but the fifth Curtiss went straight in wide open. We all were watching, and it was a sad day for Oakland.

Despite the occasional sobering incident, I still wanted to fly, and shortly after my purloined solo in the Monoprep, I finally got my pilot's license. I was sixteen years old. Mildred Rose threw a coffee party to celebrate, inviting the people from Boeing Air Transport, who shared the hangar with us. I had been helping their mechanics with twenty hour checks and was hired to wash their mail planes, so we had become quite friendly. One Saturday afternoon not long after that momentous event, Jack Knight, one of BAT's mail pilots, came into the Metro section and asked if Frank or anyone else around could make a flight for him. He said he felt like he had food poisoning and was in no condition to fly the mail to San Jose. I was alone, everybody else in the hangar having gone to the same party the Boeing gang was attending. After we had exhausted all other possibilities, I ventured, "Do you think I could make the flight for you?"

Sick as he was, he started to laugh, but he was desperate. We went

*Franklin Rose (left) with a Mr. Brown and Varney Air Lines Stearman C-4-E, Bay Airdrome, early thirties.*

out to the Boeing 40-B with its new Pratt & Whitney Wasp "B" engine and I climbed into the cockpit and ran through all the starting procedures with Jack watching carefully. Finally he asked, "Do you have a helmet and goggles?" Of course I did! "Go get them. I'm going to take a big chance."

I got the helmet and goggles and returned to the airplane, listening very hard and trying to memorize his instructions. "Take your time taxiing this bird; the gear is close together and in a cross wind she'll easily ground loop. She has good brakes. In flight she's heavy on controls but she'll let you know in plenty of time if she approaches stall. And she doesn't float, so on your landing come in slightly nose high and put her down nose high without trying to three-point her. They'll be waiting for you, so don't shut down the engine. Let them unload the mail and you get away as fast as you can without talking to them. Maintain 1900 rpm on cruise and follow the bayshore home. Okay, Kid, get rolling!"

Jack waved me off and I taxied slowly to the end of the field, getting the feel of the controls, and turned into the wind. My heart was pounding as I gradually opened the throttle. The tail came up, and without any more help from me she was airborne.

Man, this was heaven. Even in a climb she handled like a baby buggy. Any sluggishness I might have felt at first disappeared when we leveled off. From Jack's description I easily found the San Jose airport, which had plenty of length but was known for a slight cross wind. Over the end of the field I cut power and raised the nose. The bird held steady as I touched down with the slightly tail high position as instructed.

The mail truck was waiting. With barely a glance at me the crew climbed into the mail pit and unloaded the bags. "Hey, you were a little late, weren't you?" someone said as they dropped off the plane. I didn't answer, swung the plane around, and took off for Oakland.

On the way back I was more relaxed and started to look around the cockpit. I noticed that on each side of the instrument panel were two small cranks labeled "Landing Lights," with a switch at the side. I turned on the left one, and as the wing tip light lowered to offer more wind resistance I saw the bird swing to the left. When I lowered the right one she straightened out. This was fun, so I kept on course to Oakland by raising and lowering the lights.

When I landed and taxied up to the BAT hangar, Jack was anxiously waiting for me and feeling a lot better. I told him about the experiment with the lights. He laughed. "You picked up on that pretty fast. We all use this system to keep on course. And by the way, your landing was real good."

The compliment was payment enough, but the following week Jack gave me twenty dollars for making the flight to San Jose. It was the first time anybody paid me for flying, and as far as I know, the U.S. Post Office Department never found out that a teenage kid had flown the mail that Saturday afternoon.

*Walter Varney's favorite picture of himself, a sketch by San Francisco artist Bob Palow, 1931, presented by Varney to the author.*

CHAPTER 3

# The Education of a Ramp Rat

THE COMPLETION OF THE Posey tube under the Oakland Estuary in 1928, connecting Oakland to the island of Alameda, and the San Francisco Bay Airdrome privately developed there in 1930, brought radical changes to the Eastbay aviation. Citing a lack of cooperation by the Oakland Port Commission, Maddux Air Lines and Western Air Express moved to the Bay Airdrome, and were followed by a number of other operations.

Ours was one of them, but under a new name. Metro had been bought by the already legendary Walter T. Varney, whom I would know very well in later years, and the named changed to Varney Air Lines. Walter had sold Varney Air Transport and its lucrative Western mail contract for a couple of million dollars to the new United Airlines. He stayed with United for a while, but in his typically restless way, left to start another operation.

It would be difficult to exaggerate Walter's role in the development of West Coast aviation. Perhaps the very fact that he came to it from considerable wealth contributed to the roller coaster aspects of his nevertheless notable career. His father had founded Varney and Green Advertising, later Foster & Kleiser, and when Walter had money he did things like buying the Shell Building in San Francisco, starting airlines, flying the mail, and helping bail out the Lockheed Aircraft

Corporation, always maintaining his fine reputation as a pilot. I knew him as a friend, not as an employer, at the time he didn't have money, but suffice it to say Walter always seemed to land on his feet. During World War II, for example, he had to work as an inspector at Lockheed; then at the age of sixty-five he became a test pilot for the B-17s Lockheed was building for Boeing. Not only that, Walter was a great raconteur, a fountain of aviation historical lore, and best of all a good friend.

The beloved "Green Hornet" now sported the Varney name. I was aboard when Frank Rose flew us, accompanied by five other aircraft, from the Oakland airport to Alameda seven days after the Bay Airdrome opened. Completing the very short flight, we were met and photographed by reporters from the *Oakland Tribune*, who duly noted the alarming exodus from Oakland's municipal facility.

Our new location was more convenient for me to get to; from downtown Oakland I had only to walk through the tube, which exited directly onto the Airdrome's entrance. Navy planes have been flying off the north end of Alameda for years, now, but little remains to indicate that a major private airport ever existed beneath today's fancy developments and marinas. The San Francisco Bay Airdrome ceased operation in 1941.

Initially there was one hangar, divided into three bays, plus a lobby and a restaurant. We moved into bay #2 with a nice shop and offices, sharing the hangar with the Standard Oil Company's Ford Wasp-powered trimotor and Lockheed Vega. While the company reorganized and built another hangar, Walter sent me over to the old Boeing hangar at Oakland to get some more training. I learned a lot from a real pro who worked there. I regret having forgotten his name, but we met again during the war when he was a maintenance chief at Boeing in Seattle. Later, when United Airlines set up their maintenance base at Oakland, Walter lent me to them to help out in the engine department until they could train their own mechanics. I stayed only a couple of months, but it amused me to tell people I was United's first engine overhaul man.

There was an interesting character there who didn't seem to have a specific job, but who turned up everywhere. He helped in the hangar and in the shop, sometimes doing dirty work like washing airplanes, cleaning parts, and scrubbing out on Saturdays. He asked all kinds of questions and on occasion offered good advice. Everybody liked him. Only later did we find out it was W.A. "Pat" Patterson, UAL's future president who had undertaken a self-imposed training program to find out how the airline worked. He learned the business from the ground up, and eventually put UAL on the map—and later helped ease Varney Speed Lanes out of business by spurring the development of the Boeing 247.

Foulmouth Phil, who, by now had taught me everything he knew about his two favorite subjects, didn't want to move to the Bay Airdrome. No one person could fill his shoes, so Frank Rose, whom Varney had made president of the new operation, hired a couple of new mechanics, one of them a student who worked cheap to learn, the other a friend of our bookkeeper, Everett "Andy" Anderson. The student caught on fast, but Andy's friend, unfortunately, was ill-suited to the profession. Invariably, just when he was busy groping around a customer's plane, Frank would need a twenty-hour check on a Varney plane and usually I had to do it.

I still wasn't getting paid, at only seventeen still willing to work for stick time. But having to do the other mechanic's work was beginning to rankle. Frank admitted that my engines ran smoother after the twenty-hour checks than the ones the mechanic worked on, but he couldn't get authorization from Sammy Metzger to hire another mechanic. Instead, how would I like an hour in the Comet Stearman for each twenty-hour check? That was almost as good as money. Although underpowered, the Stearman was our school ship and flew well. I accepted the deal, but it didn't help when Sammy came in and ordered me to teach the paid mechanic how to do twenty-hour checks. When I refused he offered me $10. I told him where to put it and walked away. Frank heard about it, but instead of scolding me for being rude to the boss he told me to hold my ground, and then he saw to it that I got plenty of twenty-hour checks. That translated into the coveted air time, which was more important than money at that point.

I had also acquired some additional hangar duties because, to earn extra credits to graduate ahead of my high school class, I was learning to weld in trade school. Frank was taking advantage of my new skill by having me do necessary welding when the need arose.

One day the mechanic let a customer's plane slip off a support horse and Frank asked me to repair the damage. The bottom longeron was creased beyond repair. I would have to splice in a new section. By studying the fuselage I found where they had spliced in a section at the factory. I could copy that, but in order to do it I had to cut off quite a bit more than the damaged area, and replace it with a five-point cluster weld.

Everything was cut, trimmed, and ready to go when the ever vigilant Edison E. "Monty" Mouton showed up and saw what I was doing. Monty was the highly respected Department of Commerce Aeronautics Branch supervising inspector for the Western states. He called Frank over and asked, "Does The Kid have a license?" Frank said I didn't yet, but that he was supervising the work. Monty said "That won't do. This is a major structural member and all he has is a pilot's license." Frank told him there was nobody else in the area who could do this type of work, so Monty said he'd stick around and watch, but first I had to make a cluster weld so he could judge my ability.

I cut up some old tubing and made a cluster, Monty standing over me wearing welding goggles and watching every move. When I finished, Monty said, "That's about the best cluster weld I've seen. Go ahead with your repair, but call me for final inspection."

As he signed off the repair, Monty patted me on the head and said that when I was ready to apply for my E license he'd waive the welding portion. He was as good as his word. Frank handed me two ten dollar bills, then he and Monty escorted me to the airport restaurant and bought me my first drink.

The new Varney Airlines flew to Sacramento with two Stinsons powered by the Pratt & Whitney Wasp. Walter also had just bought into the Air Ferries Company, which flew a six-mile route from Grove Street in the Oakland Estuary to Pier 5 in San Francisco, using the Loening amphibian powered by the Wright 750-h.p. Cyclone. Frank got me a weekend job as co-pilot with "Big Dick" Mitchell, who later helped start the secret Banana River project that developed into Cape Canaveral in Florida.

My only duty as co-pilot was to wind up the landing gear and wind it down again, 168 turns in each direction, and then climb out and hand the mooring lines to the men on the pier during the two-minute turn-around time. I never had much of a chance at the flight controls, but I learned a lot watching Dick handle the ungainly bird with engine blasts to control the flight rudder.

*Edison E. "Monty" Mouton, Department of Commerce aviation inspector, and Roscoe Turner, Oakland Municipal Airport, 1930.*

*Art Kennedy with Varney Air Ferries Sikorsky-39 powered by Pratt & Whitney Wasp, Jr., 1933. This aircraft replaced the Loenings after the author and "Big Dick" Mitchell ditched in San Francisco Bay.*

It was a good thing I was watching. Late one cold afternoon our engine quit as we were deadheading to Pier 5. We sat down on the water just past Yerba Buena Island, where Treasure Island is now. Dick jumped out onto the pontoon and opened the cowl to look for the problem while I tried to keep her headed into the wind. As good a mechanic as he was a pilot, Dick found the trouble in a matter of minutes and repaired it. By this time we had been swept north to well abreast of Alcatraz Island, and were screaming toward the Golden Gate in the strong ebb tide.

These birds had only a hand inertia starter, so Dick called for the crank, which, as bad luck would have it, the guy at Oakland had forgotten to put aboard after starting us. Taking off his shoes and pants, Dick got in front of the engine, hollering "Give her lots of prime and switch off. I'm going to hand-pull this bastard. If we don't get out of here it'll be curtains for both of us!"

He was standing face to face with the big Cyclone with no place to go if it started. "What are you going to do if this thing starts?" I shouted.

"Hell, just give me a chance. If it coughs at all don't lose it. If she keeps going, I'll have to take a bath. Try to come around and pick me up. If you can't pick me up, head for the beach."

I yelled "contact!" and watched the big three-bladed prop start to move and finally cough, and as Dick fell backward into the water she took hold and ran like a dream. I tried to taxi around to get him, but the flatsided amphib, with no water rudder and fighting the wind and tide, was hard to control.

The first time around I missed by yards, and Dick pointed to the beach, trying to tell me to leave him and head for safety. I pretended not to understand, circled again, and missed again. On the third try he caught a wing pontoon and managed to haul himself up. I throttled back to complete idle, leaned out, and helped him in. He had just about had it in that cold water.

I tried to tell him how sorry I was that I missed him twice, but he grabbed me hard and said, "You little bastard, I love you! When I hit that water I was sure I'd had my last flight. How you even managed to get near me was a damn miracle."

It took us more than an hour to taxi the three miles to base. Dick spent two days in the hospital. When he came out he took me to the famous flyer's hangout called the Fly Trap in San Francisco, where he and his pilot friends told the bartender they'd take him apart if he threw me out for being underage, and proceeded to get me very drunk.

After this incident Walter Varney replaced the Loening with a Sikorsky S-39. With Varney's name painted on the fuselage, they used it until the Bay Bridge linking San Francisco to Oakland was completed in 1936 and the air service was discontinued.

Varney Airlines was doing a land office business flying to Sacramento, but although she had plenty of power the Stinson was licensed only for a pilot and three people. They took to loading some extra passengers in the back until Monty Mouton got wind of it and warned that if he caught them at it he'd shut them down.

Frank and Walter promised to be good, but being good cost too many passengers and Walter was dissatisfied. A creative, if extravagant, businessman with full confidence in the future of aviation, he decided to buy Lockheed's new Orion.

In 1931 Walter ordered six Orions and reorganized his company, adding a Los Angeles-to-San Francisco route and calling it "Varney Speed Lanes." Franklin Rose remained as president, and Varney availed himself of the free advice of a financial wizard from the East Coast named Robert E. Gross, who with his brother Courtland had founded the Viking Flying Boat Company. Gross managed to reign in Varney's extravagance and finally produce a profit. Later he succeeded Lloyd Stearman as president of Lockheed after he and other investors, including Walter Varney, picked up the company for $40,000 in bankruptcy court in 1932. Varney hired an old timer named Arthur F. "Pop" Wilde to head the maintenance department. I learned a great deal about airplanes from Pop.

By now I was actually being paid, $1.25 a day on Saturdays and Sundays and $1 when I came in after school. When I graduated from high school, Pop offered me $30 a month to work nights, since I had left home the day after graduation and was trying to go to college at UC Berkeley. I transferred to the night shift, but before long received four cinch notices at school, which meant I was failing four subjects and would have to take a test at $10 a subject if I wanted to pass. I couldn't afford the $40, so I dropped out of Berkeley and asked to be returned to the day shift.

We were taking care of a Stearman owned by a prominent Oakland physician named Francis Shook. Every weekend Dr. Shook went off on a trip in his Stearman, usually taking one of his nurses along, for which he got a lot of kidding. Sometimes, if nobody else was available, he took me. We'd fly down to Capitola or land on the beach near Santa Cruz, where I got my first small-field landing experience.

When Dr. Shook learned I had dropped out of school, he offered to finance my engineering studies at UC night school. While I couldn't get a degree, at least I'd acquire some valuable college-level knowledge. For almost two years I went to UC's extension classes four nights a week, taking subjects like calculus, physics, and analytical geometry. I'll always be grateful to this generous man, who loved his airplane so much that in his will he ordered it cremated at the end of the Airdrome after his death.

It was about this time that I had my first encounter with one of the most colorful females in aviation. One dreary Sunday I was in charge of the Varney hangar, not much going on, when a trimotor Bach landed and taxied up to our hangar instead of parking on the flight line. The engines shut down, so I went up to the door of the airplane to see what the pilot wanted.

Down the aisle marched a large, bull-necked woman with a frizzy hairdo. Instead of the pants most female pilots wore, she was dressed in an elegant suit with a skirt. She jumped out and said, "Hey, Bud, tell me where I can take a pee, quick!" I was shocked, but smartassedly answered "Lady, the quickest is where you are." She looked at me and then looked around to see if anybody was watching. "I haven't time to jaw with a punk kid," she said, and with that she lifted up her skirt and I ran like hell.

She made a phone call and then told me to gas up, paying for it in cash from a big roll of bills. Then she climbed back into the bird, stopped suddenly and yelled, "Damn! I forgot the starter on my left motor is out. It has to be started by hand. You're too small for that; isn't there anybody around with muscle that knows how to pull through a prop?"

I said, "Look, lady, I may be small and a punk but I'm a mechanic and that Kinner out there isn't that hard. Get your big fanny into the pit and I'll start it for you."

The Kinner was only a five cylinder engine and not too far from the ground. I pulled her through several times, yelled "contact!" and the engine started the first time. The pilot leaned out the window. "You'll do, Bud! When you grow up come to L.A. and look up Pancho Barnes." With that she threw me a silver dollar, started the other two engines and took off.

I saw a lot of Pancho Barnes later on, and had reason to agree with other flyers that she may have been a tough cookie, but she was a good friend to anybody she liked.

By this time I was doing a variety of jobs for Varney: repairing wooden aircraft, patching fabric, painting, and welding, in addition to mechanical work. When Walter was notified that the first of his new Orions was ready, he took me to Burbank on the delivery flight to learn all I could about the new retractable gear before we brought her home. He flew Frank and me down in the Green Hornet, landed at the Lockheed field, and taxied up to the old china factory at Turkey Crossing. There sat that beautiful new Orion. She was painted white with red trim. "Varney Speed Lanes" was lettered on the side and the number NC 12222 on her tail. On the cowling was her name, "South Wind." It was the most beautiful aircraft I had ever seen.

Our bird was all ready to go, but they had another one still on jacks in the hangar, where a great guy named Harvey Christen gave me some training on the retractable gear. At that time, Harvey was mechanic, stock man, delivery boy and hangar cleaner at Lockheed, but eventually he became a vice president in charge of the company's quality control. We were to renew our acquaintance during World War II when I worked at the Lockheed plant, and happily made contact again during research for these memoirs more than forty years later. Still active in retirement, he is the lone survivor of the original pre-1932 Lockheed group, and a fountainhead of aviation history.

The Orion had interesting beginnings. During innumerable later conversations in our home about his aviation experiences, Walter Varney told me that it was he and Lockheed designer George Prudden who needled the company about converting the new low wing Sirius into a passenger plane with retractable landing gear. The Sirius was a two cockpit open with a fixed gear and streamlined pants. Otherwise it was a Vega with the wing on the bottom, the same model Charles and Anne Lindbergh flew on their route surveys for Pan American.

On Walter's Orions, the cockpit was up front, like the Vega, the pilot's feet straddling the magneto housing on the firewall. A twenty-

*Lockheed mechanic Harvey C. Christen with Amelia Earhart's red Vega, 1929*

*Recent photo of Harvey C. Christen. Retired as Lockheed vice president.*

*Passengers debark from Varney Speed Lanes Orion, Bay Airdrome, Alameda, California, early thirties. Note earlier "Varney Speed Lines" stairway from predecessor line, sometimes confused with the "Speed Lanes" that flew Orions.*

gallon fuel tank was placed behind the pilot's head. The cabin held six passengers, with a baggage compartment aft. This was the last of the great line of wooden ships built at the Lockheed plant, and followed the Vega, Sirius, and Altair as the fourth Lockheed aircraft named after a celestial body. With the Orion was born the first U.S. passenger airliner with a successful hydraulically operated retractable gear.

It had taken us four hours to fly to Burbank in the Stearman. Walter flew the Orion back to Alameda in one hour and fifty-six minutes. When he put the Orions into service, Walter advertised the flight time as an hour and fifty-eight minutes to L.A., with a ten cent refund for every minute they were late. Passengers seldom got a refund. One time the Orion flew from Los Angeles to Oakland in sixty-five minutes.

It's no wonder air travel between Los Angeles and Oakland caught on so fast. By automobile the trip between the two cities took fourteen to sixteen hours over the old Grapevine highway. Overnight trains took twelve hours. A boat trip was fourteen hours long.

Other Bay Area airlines were taking nearly four hours, at best, to fly to Los Angeles, so Varney Speed Lanes was cleaning up with the Orion. Maddux had the "Tin Goose" trimotor Ford powered by Wasps. Western Air Express tried the Fokker 32, a four-engine bird with the new Pratt & Whitney Hornet. Two engines were mounted in tandem under each wing, one puller and one pusher. But this engine had, among other bugs, a problem with cylinder head cooling and consequently rarely completed a trip without one or two engines out. It messed up the schedule so badly they finally abandoned the bird, and one of them finished life at a Hollywood gas station.

Pitcairn Airlines' trimotor Stinsons powered by the Lycoming engine couldn't compete, either. Bach Airlines' wooden trimotor Bach, powered by two Kinners and a Wasp in the nose, was light and fairly fast, but not fast enough. Boeing Airlines flew the Boeing 80 with three Wasps, and then the Boeing 80A, which had three Hornets and needed three tails for controllability. It was the most comfortable aircraft of them all, had a toilet aboard, and carried the first female attendants to take care of passengers. But even the 80A was not as fast as the Orion.

Varney was a clever promoter and never failed to take advantage of his Orions' superior performance. He ordered his pilots to circle their competitors in the sky as closely as possible before continuing and always to buzz the control towers at both ends of the route. He had widely advertised Varney Speed Lanes as having the first commercial aircraft with retractable landing gear and the public loved to see the sleek airliner pass over with the gear neatly tucked in. Not until the advent of the pressurized DC-6 was the Varney Speed Lanes speed record broken in West Coast commercial aviation.

We were carrying so many passengers that we had to put on double and triple headers. The other airlines were hurting, but were unable to buy any planes from Lockheed because Walter's deal stipulated that Lockheed would not sell Orions to competitors on the West Coast.

With all this business, the maintenance department was growing. I worked full time for $35 a month, breaking my tail trying to make good. I was supporting myself and helping out my parents, and gave up a lot of more interesting things to buy tools with my own money. In my free time I manufactured or modified tools for special applications.

Pop Wilde and I got along well, once he got used to my way of solving problems. Early on, Pop told me to do something about the bad odor in my lean-to welding shack, which the neighborhood dogs had appropriated for a pit stop.

I didn't know what to do about it until one of our electricians gave me an idea. I dug up the ground surrounding the offending corner and placed a copper screen on it, lightly covered with dirt. Then I wrapped another copper screen around the wall about six inches up from the ground. These I hooked up to the nearly 110 volt outlet, kept the dirt damp, and waited for something to happen.

A few days later we heard an unearthly scream from the welding shop and Pop shot out of the back with his fly open, hanging on to his dong for dear life—the first and only victim of his own orders!

I felt terrible about it and was sure he'd fire me. "It wasn't your fault, Kid," he said. "I had no business pissing in there, and I didn't bother to check with you about how you were going to get rid of the smell. It was pretty ingenious!' When he got out of the hospital Pop immediately enclosed the welding shack and put in a proper cement floor.

But from then on, Pop never gave me a job to do without asking how I was going to do it. I missed him when he moved to a better job on the East Coast.

Varney finally got fed up with paying Pacific Aeromotive Company in Oakland for engine overhauls and decided we could do it cheaper in an overhaul shop of our own, which we created by closing off the rear of the hangar. Al Notley, who had been a field service engineer for Comet and later became a C.A.A. inspector, ran the shop with me as his assistant.

We had overhauled only two engines before Al was promoted to supervisor of the maintenance department and Frank put me in charge of the shop. I felt the responsibility keenly, but got some expert training from the Pratt & Whitney representative from Los Angeles, Wilbur Thomas. Wilbur was a full-blood Sioux who drove up from L.A. in a Pierce Arrow and always made me help him clean its engine before he would do anything for me in the shop. He turned up subsequently in aviation history as the Pratt & Whitney man who was on the field when Amelia Earhart aborted her take-off in Honolulu during the first round-the-world attempt.

Under Wilbur's tutelage we built a test stand on the back of an old truck, and since Al was too busy to help me very much, he insisted that I follow the P&W overhaul manual to the letter. I didn't want the other mechanics to know that I had to use the book, so I would lock the shop door when I needed to look up something. The mechs had to knock to get in, and I would quickly close the book and put it in a drawer, pretending to be busy at something else until they left.

Eventually they caught on, and I'd open the door to find nobody there. I drilled a hole in the door, mounted a Plews gun filled with water and heavy cheap perfume, and fixed up a lever attached to a string hanging over the engine stand. When the next knock came I yanked the string and my invention worked like a charm. There was a yell and some mighty cursing, and who should be standing in the doorway but my boss, Al Notley. I had done it again!

Al finally laughed about it—after I helped him prove to his wife that he hadn't been out with another woman. The incident seriously jeopardized his marriage, which I didn't learn for some time and even then didn't understand fully what my kid trick had done to him.

We now had a lot of new machinery, but I didn't know as much about using it as I wished. I asked for Saturday afternoons off to attend machine shop courses at the Polytechnic School in Oakland. I couldn't convince Al and Frank that nobody really knew what our machines could do, but Walter Varney, who seldom involved himself in personnel matters, had different ideas.

"What in hell's the matter with you guys?" he said. "The Kid wants to help us and he's at an age when you don't stop him from trying. As owner of this damn airline I'm not going to ask your opinion this time. The Kid goes to machine shop school and if necessary you can hire temporary help for the engine shop until he finishes. And that's final!"

It was a relatively complete course for those days. I finished second in the final exams, and at work wound up with almost more responsibility than I had time for in the hangar and engine overhaul shop.

In 1932 Varney Speed Lanes experienced one of the weirdest tragedies in aviation history. It occurred on a winter night when Jack Evans, an excellent pilot, was flying an Orion in from Burbank. With heavy ground fog closing around San Leandro south of Oakland, the tower tried in vain to advise Jack of fast deteriorating visibility. He finally called the tower and said he had lost all contact and was turning around to try to land at Lodi if it was still open. Altimeters then were not the precision instruments they are now, and before long the tower got a call from the police that an airplane had crashed in San Leandro. I had taken a girlfriend to the movies, and found out about it when an usher was sent into the theater with a message for me to report to the airdrome immediately.

The following day I helped Al Notley comb the field for engine parts. We found wingtip marks cutting through a hayfield, apparently made while Jack was in a turn. As he straightened out he hit an outhouse and then plowed into the main house where a family of ten were having a late supper. The eleventh member of the family was coming up the front porch. He was knocked into the street uninjured, but everyone else was killed, along with Jack and his two passengers.

It happened on the thirteenth of the month. Thirteen people were killed. The house number was 1313. The tail number of the airplane was NC 12226, which adds up to thirteen. One press report claimed that thirteen "thirteens" were involved.

While Varney Speed Lanes was prospering, other West Coast airlines were having problems. TWA's four-engine Fokkers were uncomfortable, noisy, and unreliable; finally the public began to make fun of the frequent failures to complete a trip. With a full load they couldn't even get over the mountains and had to fly the coast.

Adding one especially ludicrous note, airline mergers changed TWA's name to Transcontinental Western Air Transport, but for only a brief time. Californians did not appreciate the resulting unhappy acronym on the side of a public conveyance, so it was quickly changed back to TWA. It was not one of the airline's proudest moments and is seldom mentioned in airline histories, but I certainly remember being asked to find some white paint for the TWA man so he could paint out that last "T" on the F-32 Fokkers at the Bay Airdrome. They had received notice that if one more bird arrived in Burbank with the new abbreviation on it, the airline would be fined for obscenity.

UAL was still flying the old Boeing biplanes but the speed was about the same as the others and Varney Speed Lanes still carried the cream of the loads. Although Walter charged slightly higher fares, the time difference gave him the passengers.

Like everyone else, United wanted to buy Orions, but Varney had locked that up. So they turned to Boeing, which had an all metal fixed gear twin engine B-9 bomber on the drawing boards. United began looking at it and realized that even converted for passengers it would be slower than the Orion, which in fact was faster than the new Boeing pursuit ships—the Army's P-12 and the Navy's F-4B4.

But they forged ahead, United insisting that any new ship should have retractable landing gear. Boeing protested. The landing gear on the tail dragger would have to be high enough to give prop clearance for the big Hornet engines they planned to use. Nevertheless, they went to work designing the bird for passengers while United's Pat Patterson talked to Pratt & Whitney and Hamilton Standard about power plants with smaller propellers.

It was clear that the Hornet would consume too much fuel for the small difference in airspeed it gained. They decided to gear down the engine and Hamilton designed a smaller diameter three-bladed propeller. Thus was developed the highly successful Wasp S1H1G, which used the standard WASP power section with a ten-to-one blower and three-to-one nose gear reduction.

United returned to Boeing with the new prop diameter so they could shorten the gear and make it retractable. What came out of that project was the famous Boeing 247. Carrying enough fuel for more than 500 miles, it could accommodate ten passengers, four more than the Orion. UAL got a firm commitment from Boeing for the first twenty 247s, which they began to deliver early in 1933.

Boeing staged a massive advertising campaign for the new airplanes and captured the public's imagination with their newly designated registered nurses, which they now called "stewardesses." Long before it actually affected Varney Speed Lanes, however, Walter saw the handwriting on the wall. Abruptly and without fanfare, he closed down the airline.

The public was in an uproar. We were flying double and triple headers, and the rest of the airlines put together didn't have enough seats for travelers fast becoming accustomed to airplane travel. Businessmen tried to buy Walter's Orions, but he wouldn't sell them. Lockheed had more orders than they could fill from Braniff in the Midwest and Swissair in Europe. They had added flaps and made her a beautiful short field bird as well as a fast one. Consequently, there was consternation in the airline business until Boeing was able to speed up production of the 247s.

The three years I spent at the San Francisco Bay Airdrome were exciting for an airplane-happy teenager, but they were even more important for the great impact on my life and my thinking. As I grew up and became proud of my small part in the historic Varney operation, I finally shed the nickname "The Kid." Mildred Rose was the first to call me "Arthur" when the two of us had a forced landing and I figured out an unconventional but effective way to get the Kinner engine running so we could get back to Alameda in one piece. We were very late, however, and Frank's concern for Mildred showed us all how much he loved her. He didn't say much to me, but from then on I was "Art" to him.

Frank's confidence in putting me in charge of my first engine shop set my feet on the right path to a good reputation in aviation. Here I learned important basic lessons about following directions and accepting instruction. It was in that shop at the Bay Airdrome that I made most of my mistakes and got well tenderized with some much needed humility, shocked to discover that I was not the greatest mechanic at the airport. Nor the greatest flyer.

In spite of the hangar high jinks, which also taught me to laugh at the practical jokes that once infuriated me, some events at the Bay Airdrome were quite sobering. When a welding accident started a bad fire in the hangar, two of us had to pull my friend Nick Hansen face down across a floor enveloped in flames fed by oil. He was terribly burned and scarred, but survived to become a top technician for Bendix West Coast. Our paths crossed a number of times throughout the years in the most unlikely places. Nick was a fine human being, always ready to hash over our technical problems or share in the horseplay.

While I may have played as hard as I worked, I never lost sight of my one serious goal. When I was nineteen I decided to apply for my engine license. Monty Mouton thought I was too young, but nevertheless gave me a study sheet and said that if I passed the written test he'd give me the practical and see how I did. He already knew I could weld, and had witnessed my cable splicing, wood work, and doping and painting.

I studied hard for two weeks. Then Monty put me in a room by myself and gave ten questions to answer in eight hours. Any that I didn't finish would be held against me. In those days you didn't have the luxury of answering multiple-choice questions. They gave you essay questions, such as "What is friction?" and "Describe how you overhaul a carburetor." You really had to know the material to get it done, and fortunately I was three-quarters finished with the last question when he called time and sent me home.

Three days later he telephoned to say I had passed the written, and early the next morning he appeared in the shop and spent the whole day watching me repair and assemble the engine I was working on. At the end of the shift he asked a lot of technical questions, which I was able to answer. Finally he shook my hand, a little reluctantly I thought, and said I'd made it.

Three weeks later I received the Department of Commerce's E license #12001, one of the lowest numbers still active today. That has been confirmed by the FAA, which for some reason is unable to tell me if it's *the* lowest number. In another ten years or so the CAA would add an unrestricted airframe license (A&E), and in 1956 my license was changed to read Aircraft and Powerplant (A&P), the highest category today, meaning the holder can work on engine accessories and anything in front of the firewall.

But January 3, 1933, was the greatest day of all. I had become, at last, one of aviation's anointed, licensed to maintain, repair, and overhaul airplane engines. "The Kid" finally had become a real ramp rat. Walter Varney celebrated by giving me a raise.

CHAPTER 4

# Leaving the Nest

THE DAY AFTER he shut down Varney Speed Lanes, Walter bought a used Lockheed Vega and started over again with Capitol Airlines, flying from Mills Field in San Francisco to Sacramento. I was sent up to Sacramento to serve as the mechanic for a group of old-time Varney pilots—George Buck, Joe Taft, Jack Bilby, Jess Hart, and Avery Black. Joe was stone deaf, but he never had any trouble understanding you when the engines were roaring full blast.

For the first time in my life I was on my own. Work kept me too busy to get into much mischief. Sundays were free, however, so I could make some extra money selling tickets for a barnstormer named Jerry, whose last name, unfortunately, has disappeared from my memory bank. Jerry had a fine J-5 Pitcairn and he liked to use it, which is why he and I stumbled into the agriculture business.

The winter was severe, with unusually heavy rains and lots of flooding. North of Sacramento the mud was too deep for farmers to get their equipment into the fields. One of them, a friend of Jerry's from Gridley in the Sacramento Valley, hired him to fly over his fields to see if there was any way he could get in to plant rice.

He returned from the survey quite despondent. Trying to cheer him up, Jerry half jokingly suggested that he could plant the rice from the air. His friend looked at him as if he were nuts and started to walk away, but turned back and said, "Hey, maybe you have something. Even a small crop would be better than nothing. I'm willing to gamble if you are."

"How about it, Art?" said Jerry. I didn't know the first thing about sowing by air nor anything about rice, but we decided to give it a try. Jerry told his friend to get the rice to the nearest place we could land, and we would dream up something.

First we had to figure out how to throw seeds out of an airplane. We decided to remove the dual controls and cut a hole in the floor of the Pitcairn's large cockpit. I would sit in one corner and we'd put the sacks of seeds around the sides. When Jerry signaled, I would dump out the seeds. It was too noisy to shout, especially with my head down in the rice sacks, but if we cut a hole between the cockpits Jerry could shove a broomstick through it and jab me in the back when it was time to begin pouring.

Neither of us could find anything wrong with this approach, so we got to work and modified the Pitcairn.

As soon as Jerry's friend found a landing strip, we flew up and helped his crew load six sacks of seed into the cockpit. I opened one and got quite a shock. They weren't seeds at all; they were more like little twigs!

The farmer had hired several men to stake out his fields with flagged poles. As we approached the flags, Jerry gave me a thumbs up and circled for the first run. I slit open a bag, got ready over the hole and started pouring when Jerry jabbed. I couldn't see through the twigs flying back in my face, but I kept pouring until we finished one line and Jerry would jab again to tell me to stop. Finally I signaled we were out of "seeds" and we returned to base.

My back was so sore that I made Jerry pad the communications system before we took off with another load. Airborne again, we started dumping, with Jerry taking much tighter turns on the return run. We made four flights that day and three on Sunday. The following weekend we dumped nine loads. Jerry's friend was delighted. He had accomplished in two weekends what would have taken three weeks on the ground.

Now all we had to do was wait for the results. I had almost forgotten about it until after I was transferred back to Mills Field in San Francisco and got a letter from Jerry with a check for a hundred dollars as my share. The crop we had sown was the best they'd ever had. He now had several contracts with farmers in the Sacramento area, experimenting with sowing wheat. I never found out how successful that was. Further interest in the project was obscured by my elation at getting the check. When it arrived, I had exactly ten cents to my name, and was debating whether to have coffee and a doughnut for dinner, or just coffee and save the rest for breakfast.

It was while I was working in Sacramento that I cracked up an airplane for the first and only time. It happened up near Gridley, when I was flying a friend's Robin, the two of us dinking around just for the hell of it. I was watching the altimeter when we approached the field for landing since fog had closed in and outside we were ceiling zero. But I forgot that the altimeter was set for San Francisco Bay instead of Gridley's higher elevation. Thinking I had 3000 feet below me and would break into the clear, I confidently came down in a powered stall condition and flew smack into a haystack. The fog was on the ground! The plane slid off the haystack into the field and, after we climbed out, he and I thought it was so funny we sat there and laughed while the airplane burned up. Nevertheless it was a stupid and potentially fatal error, and the last time anything like that happened when I was at the controls.

I stayed with Capitol Airlines until Al Notley, now working for Walter Varney in Burbank, asked me to join him there. Walter had a new project going. He had started a little airline called Lineas Aéros Occidentales with a contract from the Mexican government to fly mail to Mexico City. Excited at the prospect of rejoining the old Speed Lanes gang, I immediately booked the *H.F. Alexander* night sailing to Long Beach. I had just enough money to buy a little breakfast and then hitchhike to Burbank with two heavy tool boxes and a small suitcase.

Al met me at the dock, much to my surprise and almost tearful gratitude. He had correctly guessed that I would be short of funds.

While we were driving out to Union Air Terminal, he admitted that they were more interested in my tools than me, and warned me not to lend tools to anybody. Although he had a good deal with Pacific Airmotive Company, located just across the field from the hangar, and wouldn't need to overhaul engines, Al said I wasn't to worry about keeping busy. They needed a welder to repair cracks in the landing gears, which were taking a beating on rough Mexican fields. Furthermore, the government had informed Varney that his new airline did not have enough licensed mechanics on the payroll.

I filled the bill on all counts, and suggested as the conditions of employment that Al would back me up and not allow anyone to borrow my tools, and that I would be assigned to any job where those tools were needed. When you're twenty years old, have an E license and excessive self-confidence, you do things like that. I remember wondering why Al smiled a little as he agreed to the conditions.

As it turned out, my two big Kennedy boxes contained the only tools at the hangar. I was swamped with work, putting in more time than the rest of them for the same pay they were getting.

Finally I went to Al and suggested that either he buy tools for the others or pay me overtime. Walter Varney walked in during the conversation and Al said, "What in hell am I to do with this high-handed kid?" For the second time Walter intervened on my behalf. "I think he has a legitimate gripe," he said. "I've been here at night when he was the only one working. And he hasn't delayed one plane." One thing Walter was adamant about was taking off on schedule.

Then he told us they were going to be flying into three more rough Mexican fields and could expect a lot more gear trouble, but he didn't want to invest in too many tools until he saw how the mail contract worked out.

"You'd better do something for him," Walter said. We finally agreed to $5 a month more and a meal ticket at the Pullman Cafe near the Del Monte Hotel, where I was living.

With the raise I was making only $85 a month, but there were some perks, including less overtime and a permanent client on the side. Paul Lukas, the movie star, was a tennis pal of Walter Varney's. When Paul needed somebody to take care of his Stearman C-4E, Walter had suggested me. Not only did I service the plane, but convinced Paul that after each major service it was best that I test hop the bird. Sometimes I found it necessary to test hop it more than once, and at least for an hour. I got some nice air time with Paul footing the gas bill, but I suspect he knew what I was up to.

For the first time since achieving adulthood I was finding time for a personal life, and good things were beginning to happen. Shortly after moving to Burbank I went to the public library one evening and struck up a conversation with an attractive girl at the check-out desk. She introduced herself as Polly Simon (although she later admitted her real name was Mary Ethel). She was working her way through UCLA, majoring in archaeology. I asked her out, and before long we were keeping steady company. One of many things we had in common was a love for tennis. Polly was a superb athlete, and I was fairly good, having grown up across the street from Don and Lloyd Budge in Oakland. Our house had the only dining room table big enough for ping pong, so the Budge boys spent a lot of time there. I played tennis with them from the age of nine until Donnie got too good for the neighborhood gang.

When Paul and Walter, an avid tennis player to the end of his life, learned that Polly and I were more than passable players, they began to take us to Palm Springs for weekend games with the movie folk. Paul put us up at the Desert Inn, where we played doubles with his Hollywood friends, Claudette Colbert and Wendy Barry among them. It was a heady atmosphere for a couple of barely middle-class kids. Our hosts' generosity paid additional dividends later on when some of the stars bought airplanes and remembered how Paul's plane was always polished and ready to go when he wanted it.

Polly took great interest in my work and often helped ready the airplanes for these clients. She was good at anything she ever tried. Eventually she earned her degree in archaeology and graduated Phi Beta Kappa from UCLA. Sometimes it was hard for me to believe that this gifted girl could be interested in an airplane mechanic, but whatever the chemistry was, we got on extraordinarily well.

At Walter's Lineas Aéros Occidentales in Burbank, one of the high priority jobs was pulling long thorns out of airplane tires. Picked up on Mexican landing strips, they were quite a problem for the airline. This unpleasant and tedious job often went to men who couldn't get jobs elsewhere. Hard times had no class system. Jackie Coogan, the former child movie star, and Brandt Goldsworthy, my boyhood friend from Oakland who later became successful in the plastics business, both labored in that sticky field at one time or another.

Thorns were only a minor nuisance, however, compared to the dog-eat-dog competition among the airlines flying to Mexico. Anything was considered fair as long as you didn't get caught. Pan American, in particular, played very rough.

We were flying passengers and mail in five Orions left over from the Varney Speed Lanes fleet, and Pan American's Mexican subsidiary was flying the same route without a mail contract, using Razorback Fairchilds and two 6000 cabin Travel Airs, both powered with Wasp engines. Their cruising speed was a little over 110 miles mph, but we were faster and maintained almost a monopoly on the business.

Unsuccessful in getting Lockheed to sell them some Orions or even Vegas, Pan Am resorted to creative trickery to get us in trouble with Mexican and U.S. Customs.

They tried smuggling dope, fruit, and meat aboard our birds, but this didn't work because Walter always had a couple of Pan Am employees on his payroll, and would hire a special agent to go through our aircraft on the last stop before landing at the border in Nogales. The customs people, accompanied by a PAA agent, had an amazing way of going directly to the parcel, suitcase, or person from which our agent had just removed planted contraband. After a while Pan Am gave up without ever learning how we were staying ahead of their game.

Walter's people remained vigilant, however. One day as our bird taxied toward the wooden hangar at Mazatlán, one of our mechanics noticed an old Razorback parked by the hangar with the engine at high rpms and the stick tied back. Because the ropes tied to the blocks seemed unusually long, he traced them to the back of an old truck, where a Mexican sat behind the wheel.

Suspicious, the mechanic ran to the Fairchild as our plane came up in front of it, and hit the tail just as the truck moved, the force jamming one block so that it did not come out clean. Instead of hitting our plane, the Razorback turned into the hangar, crashed, and burned. PAA's new Travel Air inside was destroyed. Varney had only to observe the subsequent investigation with some amusement.

Knowing PAA wouldn't be discouraged, Varney personnel stayed suspicious of anything that went on in Mexico. At one of the smaller fields they had to fill up with gasoline from five-gallon cans. One day Jess Hart got out to stretch his legs and thought it strange that he didn't recognize anybody on the gas crew. Mail pilots always carried guns. Jess pulled his out as the first tin was being handed up and said, "I don't want one drop of water or I'll blow your heads off!" The crew turned pale and the guy on the wing took off the lid and smelled the contents before he poured. The fellow opening the tins on the ground sniffed each one before he passed it up.

A number of cans stayed on the ground. Jess verified that they held water, picked up one of the cans, and marched the crew into the PAA office at gunpoint. Making a great show of cocking the gun, he ordered them to pour the contents on top of the manager's desk. Then he went around the desk, poured some more over the stupefied manager and told him it was a present from Walter Varney to the president of PAA, and he hoped it would clean up all misunderstanding.

From then on, gassing crews worked under a loaded pistol and there were no further incidents with water in our fuel.

When Lockheed came out with the Electra in 1934, money was tight and they had trouble selling it. Walter, who had supplied half of the $40,000 paid for Lockheed, at last loosened his control over sales to his competition and let Lockheed make a deal with PAA, who had to put money on deposit for six birds, three more than they wanted.

The airline industry thought Walter was crazy. The Electra's speed almost could compete with the Orion and it carried four more passengers. Walter told everybody that Lockheed needed the money to keep going. The truth was that after only nine months of operation he had learned in Mexico City that his twenty-year contract wasn't worth the paper it was printed on and already had decided to close down Lineas Aéros Occidentales. He waited until PAA installed the Electras in Mexico with all their ground equipment. As soon as they were operating, he closed shop. PAA now had no competition, and, of course, they didn't need all the Electras they'd bought.

Walter sold some of the Orions to the Spaniards to use in their civil war, and sold another one to the Prince of Romania. The prince offered me a good job in Romania, but I was reluctant to leave Burbank and turned him down. I knew I didn't want to leave Burbank, but it hadn't yet dawned on me that I was falling in love with Polly.

With some of the money from his Orion sales, Walter bought two Vegas, went to Washington, D.C., and talked the government into an airmail contract between El Paso and Pueblo, Colorado. He, Thomas Fortune Ryan III, Hall Hibbard, Jess Hart, and Avery Black were starting a new airline, but the government said the Vegas had to have seven stringers in the wings. Walter's had only five.

He got the prints and we rebuilt the wings. Jim Reed, the government inspector in Burbank, confided that Walter had given me the job because I had tools and a license and was the only one of the group that he wanted to keep on. Jim had the engineering degree I did not have, and at the time I wasn't too sharp at reading blueprints. I talked him into regular visits in case I misread the prints and made a mistake, which happened once but was quickly corrected on the spot. Jimmy and I got to be good friends.

We finished the wing and Jim countersigned the log books certifying the Vega as a seven stringer. Walter then gave us a sketch for the paint job. It was to be red with white striping, with "Continental Airlines" lettered on the side. I have read other accounts that Continental Airlines began when Bob Six acquired the company from Varney in 1937. It may be true that this was the Southwest Division of Varney Airlines, as has been recorded. However, I have no doubt about Walter's instructions to us about the lettering and that it was done. By the time Six took over I was long gone from the scene.

I had to leave Burbank, after all, when we all moved to El Paso to inaugurate the new operation, which now had a fleet of three Vegas. I set up the engine shops, but I wasn't very happy. I missed Polly, who wanted to finish up at UCLA.

Walter had hired a mechanic who turned out to be exceptionally good, so I told him I wanted to go back to Burbank. He wasn't surprised. Knowing Polly and me as well as he did, and apparently much better than I did, he had foreseen the departure and hired the new man to take my place. And so, with Walter's blessing but less than excellent prospects, I returned to California. I was twenty-one, back in Burbank with my best girl, and as the Depression lingered Polly's mother found it necessary to take in a boarder. I happily moved in.

But work was hard to find. For a while I freelanced around Grand Central Airport in Glendale, recovered and painted Paul Lukas's Stearman, then was hired by American Airlines to wash their big Curtiss Condor twin engine biplanes. It was like washing down a herd of elephants and I hated it.

Next I got a night job with Orion Airlines servicing their trimotor Bachs. The pay wasn't bad, and I could supplement it by doing twenty-hour services on transient aircraft during the day.

Pancho Barnes had told me to come to L.A. and look her up when I grew up. I had grown up and gone to L.A., but I didn't have to look her up. She showed up at the Union hangar every now and then, and one day while I was washing pushrods and hangar flying with my friend Todd Oviatt, Pancho strolled in and hunched down alongside us without a word, just watching. When neither Todd nor I had anything to say, she broke the silence with, "Look fellows, shall we start talking about pussy now or just lead up to it gradually?" I'm not sure what kind of reaction she was looking for, but Todd and I broke up.

Everyone who knew her seems to have a favorite story about Pancho Barnes, *née* Florence Lowe. Polly and I had an unusual encounter one day when she asked us to drive her home from the airport, explaining that she had wrecked her car and her husband had grounded her.

We had no idea that this unabashedly raunchy female was a socialite, married then to a wealthy clergyman. We were quite unprepared to be directed to a beautiful three-story home in Pasadena. Pancho invited us in and took us on a tour of the expensively furnished house. As we returned to two large doors on the main floor, she announced, "Now I'll show you my pride and joy!" With that, she threw open the doors and ushered us into a large, high-ceilinged room with a huge bar at one end, tables and chairs scattered about, and sawdust all over the floor. The place was a mess; furthermore it looked like it had been in a fire.

Polly and I were speechless. The only thing we could think of to say was a feeble "what happened?" Pancho matter-of-factly explained that after the workmen finished building the room she instructed them not to clean it up. "When they left I sprinkled a little kerosene around, called the fire department, and tossed in a match. They put out the fire, but I told them not to mop it up. I wanted it left just the way it was. Since I don't let my drunken aviation pals in the rest of the house, we confine all our brawls in here and it just stays this way." One can only speculate about how or even if the Reverend Barnes explained Pancho to his parishioners.

Pancho Barnes went on to bigger and even more spectacular eccentricities, stirring up everyone and everything she touched in the aviation world. In spite of the later notoriety, however, she should be remembered as the outstanding pilot she really was. Pancho broke the speed record for women in 1930 and was the only woman founding member of the Associated Motion Picture Pilots. She earned and deserves that place in aviation history.

Just as things seemed to be going so well in my life, Union Airlines closed down. To add to my troubles, my old Chrysler 75 coupe started to lose power. I couldn't afford to overhaul the engine, and still owed the finance company, which was threatening to repossess it. And no jobs were in sight.

But I still had a little cash left and suggested to Polly that we take a short trip before the finance company took the car.

"Okay," she said, "but where'll we go?"

To this day I don't know why I said it, but half in jest I blurted, "Let's go to Las Vegas and get married!"

She didn't miss a beat. "Why not?"

That evening we went into Hollywood and bought a modest gold wedding ring. The next morning we told her mother we were driving to Santa Barbara and might get home late, and started out.

Stopping at every gas station along the way to fill up the boiling-over radiator, we chugged into the lazy little cowpoke town and I had to use $5 of our meager cash supply to get the radiator cleaned out. We got to the city hall minutes before it closed. A justice of the peace was handy, but we had forgotten we would need witnesses. The efficient JP walked over to the city park, pulled two bums off a bench, and for $1 apiece they witnessed our wedding ceremony.

A little dazed, we got a bite to eat and started home, arriving in Glendale at midnight, very hungry. I had exactly one dime left in my pocket. The Rite Spot on Colorado Boulevard was a favorite place of ours, so I bought one of their great ten-cent hamburgers and we sat in the car and divided it up for our wedding supper.

But we were to have a little celebration after all, thanks to Bob Bryant, one of the waiters we knew there. When Bob found out what we'd just done, he appeared with the whole crew and two more hamburgers with a beer apiece, on the house, and returned our dime, which we saved and never spent. Bob figured he couldn't get into much trouble for his generosity because he was about to quit his job and go into business for himself. Three weeks later we were his first customers at Bob's, the wooden lean-to that was the beginning of the Bob's Big Boy chain.

We returned home and spent our wedding night in our separate rooms until Polly's mother left for work the next morning. Several days went by before we finally worked up the courage to tell her that Polly had become Mrs. Arthur Kennedy.

CHAPTER 5

# Pacific Airmotive

As expected, the finance company repossessed my car, and now I had no car, no job, and a new wife. I walked out to the Union Air Terminal in Burbank and went to see Paul Mantz, who occasionally hired me when his United Air Services had a contract with a film company. Paul had no openings, but in the coffee shop that morning he had heard that Pacific Airmotive Company, just across the terminal building, might need another mechanic.

I hightailed it over and asked to speak to the manager. To my surprise I found Eddie Cooper, who had been technical manager for PAC in Oakland during my Bay Airdrome days, sitting behind the desk. He was glad to see me, but had only one opening, a dirty job in the tear-down and cleaning shack. I was happy to take it and before long had four men working for me.

Edwin O. Cooper was another of aviation's finest who had a profound influence on my career. Born in England near Farnsborough, he entered the Royal Aircraft factory there as a trade lad and graduated at seventeen. He then came to the United States and for six years worked for the U.S. Air Mail Service, where he became an expert engine mechanic. Eddie joined Pacific Airmotive in 1928, first in Los Angeles, then Oakland, and finally returned to the Southern California office. When PAC became a division of Bendix Corporation in

*Edwin O. "Eddie" Cooper as a young mechanic for the U.S. Air Mail Service with DH-4, early twenties.*

1937 Eddie remained with the company as head of their West Coast service operation, retiring in 1968. He was a fine man and good friend. Eddie's great love was the Air Mail Pioneers organization. The Eddie Cooper Collection of early air mail aviation memorabilia now has a fitting home in the San Diego Aerospace Museum at Balboa Park.

For a while I was the only licensed ramp rat at Burbank but as business grew, Eddie moved me up front into the overhaul and service section. Pacific Airmotive had a lot of regular customers among Hollywood people, and often I was sent up to the main hangar to service their planes. I had already met some of the stars on the tennis courts in Palm Springs, so by this time I was not particularly awed by the prospect of brushing shoulders with Hollywood people. Nevertheless, taking care of airplanes for the likes of Howard Hawks, Tyrone Power, and George Brent put a little edge on the work day. When air races were scheduled, a parade of American flying legends and their equally famous airplanes passed through Pacific Airmotive for servicing. Since only two of us at PAC knew how to take care of any kind of aircraft that came in, I got to know some of them as I worked on their planes.

Almost without exception they were pleasant to work with. One exception was Laura Ingalls, who flew a Lockheed Orion. I was familiar with the Orion, of course, so they assigned me to it. I'll be the first to say that Laura was a damn good pilot. In 1934 she had flown 17,000 miles from New York to South America and back, the longest flight to that date by a female pilot. Everybody gets psychoanalyzed these days, so perhaps it was because she is said to have been insecure that Laura was such a pain in the ass to work for. Whenever she wanted attention while we were working on her plane, she would imperiously blow a whistle she wore on a cord around her neck. One time, when I had her bird on jacks, she stood up in the cockpit and blew the damned whistle at me. I leaned out from under the wing and made a crude suggestion about how she could get more volume out of it. She jumped down, grabbed my arm, and marched me up to Eddie's office, all the way yelling about disrespectful mechanics.

Eddie didn't like her, either. "I'm sorry, Miss Ingalls," he said, "but I must stand by Art. I won't tolerate my mechanics being whistled for like a dog. All I'm going to do is ask him to get back to work."

"Well, I won't have him working on my plane," she said. Eddie told me to take her plane off the jacks and put it outside, and told Laura to take it away because there were no other landing gear men at PAC to finish the job.

Laura knew that nobody else at Union Air Terminal could work on an Orion. She apologized, saying she hadn't been feeling well, and asked Eddie to put me back on the job.

"We'll do it," said Eddie, "but you leave that whistle in the office and promise never to use it again." I didn't see or hear the bloody whistle again until 1978, when I saw it hanging over the bar at Barbara and Eddie Cooper's home in Van Nuys.

On the other hand, Jackie Cochran was always gracious around the mechanics. When she was getting ready for her dash to Mexico City, she brought her "Green Pickle," as we called it, to us for service. This was the large *Gee Bee* racer built by the Granville brothers and powered by a Hornet.

Jackie estimated the flight at about ten hours. One day while I was servicing the plane she came to me and said, "Art, I heard you know how to form aluminum. Is that right?" I answered that I did, and she gave me a piece of 52SO and asked me to form a piss tube to fit her.

On the spot. She wanted it for the upcoming flight. I must have turned ten shades of red, because she laughed and began to tease me. With much embarrassment I did what she asked. I must say she wore very fancy panties. When Jackie returned from Mexico she told me it worked like a charm.

But it wasn't always the very famous flyers who made our days interesting. When PAC got a call that a Kinner Fleet had a forced landing in the San Fernando Valley, I was sent out to bring it back. When I got there, one of the bystanders was laughing like hell. He told me that when he saw the plane land and ran over to help, no pilot was in sight. So he looked into the cockpit, and there was a lady, head down and stark-assed naked, trying to get into her panties.

"I asked what was wrong and she didn't seem too concerned. Just said it was so nice up there flying with nothing but a nice blue sky over her that she decided to take her clothes off. The engine had quit and she was so busy looking for a place to sit down she didn't have time to get dressed."

She was fully clothed by the time I arrived. I took the engine cowling off and found a glass fuel screen full of sand. After I cleared the lines she got in, ran up the engine several times, and took off for home.

The newspaper made a big thing out of "some woman," who actually was a lady named Bernadine King, flying around the San Fernando Valley in the buff. A couple of days later, Eddie Cooper showed me her letter of appreciation, which included a ten-dollar tip for me. Eddie couldn't help asking what I saw and I had to tell him I did see a bra on the seat in the cockpit. As a matter of fact, Bernadine King had a thing about flying around without any clothes on, which she readily admitted in a newspaper interview.

Pacific Airmotive frequently worked on Wiley Post's famous white Vega, the *Winnie Mae*. Wiley was such a congenial character that we mechanics felt we could talk to him as though he were one of us. Once I was given the job of reskinning the lower right stabilizer. When I finished, I burned in my initials and the date. Many years after, when I saw the bird hanging from the roof in the Smithsonian Air and Space museum, the initials were still there, barely distinguishable under the paint.

PAC also removed the landing gear and made a dropaway gear to diminish weight and resistance in Post's successful attempt at the world altitude record. He helped invent the pressure suit and inspired the development of the supercharger installation when the *Winnie Mae* flew from Los Angeles to Cleveland in a little over seven hours, unheard of until then, proving that he could get over 350 mph from a 200 mph aircraft by flying above 20,000 feet, and with pressurization still be comfortable. The Army was impressed. They put a pressurized cabin on a Lockheed Electra and called it the XC-35. It was a huge success, revolutionizing the airline industry.

Wiley next combined a Lockheed Orion fuselage with Sirius wings for a goodwill flight during which he and Will Rogers planned to go island hopping in Alaska and possibly continue to Japan and around the world. He wanted to install pontoons for the over-water sections of the flight, but Lockheed refused to fit the pontoons Wiley brought to them, claiming it would make the plane tail-heavy. So he bought the bird to PAC and I was told to fit the pontoons and ready them for shipping to Alaska.

I didn't know about Lockheed's stand, but the pontoons looked to me like a pile of junk. When I asked Wiley where he had picked them up, he said, "If you must know, they're off a Fairchild Razorback." I told him that, installed the way he wanted them, the pontoons would be too far aft on the Orion and would make it tail-heavy. He replied, "That's none of your business. Just do as you're told."

I lost my temper and called him a few choice names. Wiley started for me, then stopped short, laughed, and said, "Look who I'm getting mad at! You're the guy I depend on for giving my engine a good final service. Come on, Art, let's get those fittings made."

Wiley had signed a statement accepting full responsibility for the installation. Nevertheless, I was not comfortable about it and told him I was going to tell Eddie Cooper how I felt. Wiley said that was fine, but this time he wanted it done his way. Even the inspector who came to certify the plane seemed unconcerned when I pointed out that the bird looked tail-heavy. His response was that a great pilot like Wiley Post knew what he was doing.

Maybe Lockheed and I were right. After Wiley and Will Rogers were killed, the villagers giving them directions to Point Barrow reported that he didn't spend much time warming up his engine. On take-off he went into a steep climb, the engine coughed a couple of times, and slowed down from power loss. Wiley couldn't get his nose down at the slow airspeed. He went into a spin, hitting the water upside down within half a turn. I know that Wiley made the decision to use the lighter of two Pratt & Whitney engines the company suggested, because I serviced it. Perhaps he and Rogers might have survived had he chosen the heavier one.

The bodies were returned to PAC by air, and we had to unload and put them in a hearse to be taken to the funeral parlor. Eddie Cooper had received a telegram from Wiley the day before they took off from the Yukon. It said, "Everything going fine."

While work at PAC was fairly routine, I managed a little excitement during the weekends moonlighting for Paul Mantz on location for aviation films. One job was on a film featuring Jack Oakie and Virginia Bruce—I think it was *The Sky Bride*—for which an old Curtiss Falcon they had picked up from the Army was being used on the ground. It couldn't fly, but we were supposed to taxi it out as though it were taking off. It had a Curtiss D12 engine, and after a lot of work I was able to get it running, if feebly. All I had to do was run for thirty seconds with the tail up, chop the throttle, and return.

For one scene they wanted a close take of the actors alongside the wing with the engine running, but the engine noise drowned out the actors. The director asked Paul if he could keep the prop turning without the damn noise. It seemed impossible, but Paul turned the problem over to me. The engine had a taper shaft for the prop that was not splined, so we took out the woodruf key and greased it heavily, then ran a rope around the prop hub. A couple of guys out of camera range pulled the rope to make the prop turn without the engine, there was no noise, and the director was ecstatic. I'm not sure that flyers who saw that movie didn't wonder what was going on.

I'd always wanted to fly a Jenny, the Curtiss JN4-D, but got only one opportunity, during a movie being filmed at the old Van Nuys airport, and I had to cheat a little to do it. This bird had a Hisso instead of the OX-5 engine and was in wonderful condition for flying. But all I was supposed to do was put on the actor's jacket and flying goggles and taxi out of camera range with the tail up. There were so many takes that I was getting a real feel for the Jenny and wanted to fly her. Finally the man in charge of the plane came out and said the director wanted one more take, but I was to go much farther before cutting the engine. I warned him I'd have to go all the way because the Jenny had no brakes and there wouldn't be enough runway to stop. That made him nervous. He had assured the Jenny's owner that it would not be flown during the movie and he was afraid of losing future contracts with the bird.

I finally told him he'd never heard me say I might fly and taxied out to a good spot where there was lots of room and the wind right on my nose. The camera came in close and slowly backed away. I opened the throttles and after a nice long run for the cameras lifted her gently and climbed out. I leveled off, circled the field, came back in with not quite a three-point landing and returned to the set to find the director wild with joy, and wondering why I hadn't done it the first time. The plane was used in two more pictures, so everybody was happy.

I liked these movie jobs for more reasons than the money. It was an opportunity to watch Paul Mantz fly. I'll never forget shooting in Palm Springs where Paul had a Boeing 100, a sport plane adapted from the Army P-12. One of the other planes got a flat tire and when we went out to fix it Paul dived at us in the 100, upside down. He pulled out right over our heads and climbed out doing a roll on the way up. There was a flyer!

Of all the well-known individuals I worked with at PAC, Howard Hughes was larger than life. In spite of the latter-day madness that descended upon this unusual and complex man, I like to remember him as the imaginative and dedicated aviator he really was.

I got acquainted with Howard when he brought his H-1, a mean all-metal racer powered by a Pratt & Whitney twin Junior known as the R-1535, to PAC for servicing. It was a troublesome engine to work on because of the tight installation. Howard must have been pleased with the adjustments and repairs I made on it, for after a while he always asked for me to work on his plane.

At Pacific Airmotive Company what Howard wanted, Howard usually got. Because he was such a night owl, Howard often had me work on the engine at night so he could be there. He wasn't a bad mechanic, for that matter, sometimes helping me himself instead of calling in an assistant.

Howard also had the disconcerting habit of rousting me out of bed in the middle of the night to come down and run his engines. One time, when Polly and I had just moved and couldn't get a telephone right away, he came to the house and threw pebbles at our bedroom window. When he made those midnight calls, Polly would brew him a cup of coffee while I dressed, then off we'd go to the airport.

While Howard was preparing for his record-breaking Los Angeles to New York flight in 1937, he became quite agitated about the cockpit seat in the Racer, sitting in it for hours at a time testing for maximum comfort.

One day he said to me, "Nothing feels right. Maybe a cushion from a sports car is the answer. Let's go find one."

The two of us drove to Hollywood and cruised down automobile row on Sunset Boulevard, inspecting sports car cushions. We looked like a couple of bums, Howard sloppy in a decrepit slouch hat and tennis shoes with the sides slit for his bunions, and I hadn't been given time to change out of grimy overalls. As we passed the Chrysler showroom, a shiny new Imperial caught Howard's eye and we went inside. Immediately we were accosted by an indignant salesman who asked us to leave, implying that our appearance was detrimental to their display of new cars.

Howard flushed. "I might even buy one of these toys," he said. The salesman laughed. "You two get out of here before I call the cops!" I was embarrassed, but Howard was livid. He spotted the Lincoln agency across the street and hauled me into the manager's office.

Pulling out his wallet he announced, "Here is my identification. I'm Howard Hughes and I want to buy a car if you'll sell it to me right now."

"Certainly, Mr. Hughes, we can take care of that," said the manager without batting an eye.

Howard didn't stop with one Lincoln; he bought two of them. With the bills of sale in hand we returned to the Chrysler showroom, where he grabbed the salesman by the necktie and said, "Now, you pipsqueak, show me the manager's office!" He marched in with the salesman under tow, tossed down the two bills of sale and said, "See what you lost when Lord Fauntleroy here threw us out of your precious showroom? Keep those to remind you that clothes don't always make a prospective buyer!"

I heard later that he donated the two Lincolns to a convalescent facility for transporting patients. We never did find the right cushion, and finally Howard got someone at the studio to make one to fit him.

He made his historic 1938 round-the-world flight in a Lockheed Lodestar, which had the same characteristics as the B-14 bomber

Lockheed hoped to sell to the British. The early models of these birds were powered with the Wright Cyclone engine model 105, but it wouldn't lift off enough payload for the long legs Howard was planning. With the help of Curtiss-Wright, Lockheed installed the latest G-205, which was more powerful and lighter in pounds-per-horsepower than the G-105 Cyclone.

Howard made numerous experimental flights before he was confident that with the extra tanks in the fuselage and the bigger engines, he could complete each leg of his proposed trip.

As the take-off deadline approached, I gave the engines their forty-hour service and found enough metal in the oil screens to arouse suspicion of trouble. Curtiss-Wright immediately advised us that the G-205's additional power made it necessary to change the master rod bearings on both engines. They would pay for installation of their newly developed silver bearings with a lead indium flash coating. Howard was unhappy about the delay but went along with the idea.

Working night and day, we pulled both engines, removed the cylinders, and disassembled the power section to remove the crankshaft and the master rod assembly. I supervised the test run on the stand, and Howard appeared in the early morning hours with food and hot chocolate for everyone. By the time I finished running the second engine I was dead on my feet and they sent me home. I slept around the clock, but at 3:00 A.M. Howard showed up at the house to fetch me back for the final inspection and run-up.

When the weather permitted a couple of days later, Howard left for New York to begin the flight to Paris. Back in Burbank we gathered around a radio in the hangar and listened with great interest as NBC broadcast from Floyd Bennett Field, hailing Howard Hughes as "the young American aviator making only the second attempt at a non-stop flight from New York City to Paris since Charles Lindbergh's in 1927."

They interviewed Howard in the doorway of his aircraft, newly christened the *New York World's Fair of 1939*. He said he hoped his circling the globe would inspire aviators from around the world to meet at the New York World's Fair the following year in the interest of peace.

That flight, which Howard made with a crew of four between July 10 and July 14 of 1938, was a spectacular accomplishment: three days, seventeen hours, fourteen minutes and ten seconds (Lockheed's figures), a record that stood for nine years. But the hopes for peace were disintegrating, even if few of us knew it.

Someone in the U.S. Navy did know. In 1938, PAC sent me to San Diego to help get thirty-six PBYs ready for a mass flight to Hawaii. Two Pratt & Whitney reps and four mechanics from the factory in Connecticut had removed the R-1830-21 engines for modification. After they were reinstalled I was supposed to set the engines at 1000 rpms and adjust the idle mixture to produce a light blue flame from the exhaust pipe.

It might have been easy enough on one or two land planes. At the time, however, the PBY was a boat, not the PBY-5 amphibian she would become. That meant working at night—in order to see the blue flame—stretched out on a lurching narrow catwalk in the middle of San Diego Bay behind a cold prop wash. Thirty-six airplanes times two engines equaled a lot of pain.

To run the engine safely while the aircraft was moored, the Navy suggested we anchor the bird with one line and let her circle. That was fine until we got into the wakes of consecutive runs. We reduced taxi speed by running one engine at a time, but it was impossible to stay out there very long without getting seasick. The drill: start one engine, lie down on the catwalk, reach in through a mess of tubes and lines for the three mixture valves, then stretch your neck and adjust them, watching the exhaust for the blue flame indicating the proper mixture.

Despite the Navy's supply of seasick pills, I usually had to stop and upchuck just at the critical time of adjustment. I don't remember how many tools or meals went overboard, but by the time the adjustment had been made on thirty-six birds, I had lost eleven pounds.

The Navy didn't tell us they were prepared to get the flight underway at dawn the moment we finished our work. We all fell into bed and missed the take-off, which must have been a grand sight. This was the first real mass flight to Hawaii, flown the entire distance in formation. For us, the real pay-off was news of less than twenty-five gallons differences in fuel consumption among all thirty-six birds, with enough left for another two hours.

I received a nice letter of appreciation from the Navy in Washington, and a bonus from Eddie Cooper, but it took several months to get my weight back to normal.

*Pacific Airmotive Company crew, Burbank, 1935. Author identified most of the personnel either by name or what they did at PAC.*
*Front row (left to right): Bill Johnson, Ralph Ellis, Lawrence, Ed Lippus, (unidentified), Early McIntyre, Arthur Kennedy.*
*Second row: a clerk, prop man, welder, Ed Fancher, Bill Lippus, Tommy Lewis, Old Bill Fancher, carpenter, draftsman, prop shop assistant, Bob House.*
*Third row: stock man, Andy Anderson, stock control chief, Ed Adams, a salesman, Ed Sullivan, Don Shoemaker, Neil Newton, a salesman, Dutch, Pat Morrison, Al Tyson, Lee Rampton, customer relations.*
*Fourth row: Five office girls, PAC President Palmer Nicholas, five more office girls, and PAC Manager Eddie Cooper.*

By the late thirties, the aviation industry was being hard pressed to keep testing and maintenance procedures abreast of the developments in new engines. Pacific Airmotive was the West Coast representative for Pratt & Whitney and had a contract to overhaul engines for Western Air Express, which had several 247Ds. P&W sent us some experimental drawings for a new type of engine test stand they wanted to develop, and I was assigned to build a prototype for what turned out to be one of the most significant pieces of equipment yet seen in engine shops.

The cable test stand consisted of a large barrel drum to which the engine was fastened by cables instead of being attached, as had been normal up to then, to a solid ground support. Thus, it provided an anti-vibration effect to ensure accurate instrument readings. To one side of it was a soundproof shack; on the other, large windows with mirrors made it possible to see the whole engine without leaving the shack.

This may have been the first private test cell where airplane instruments were replaced by large instruments developed specifically for testing. Each had six-inch dials and were extremely precise. For a manifold indicator we built a mercury "U" tube with a sliding scale adjusted to the pressure at the time the engine was running on the test cell. We used mercury tubes also for the three oil pressure indicators and a high water tube for the fuel pressure gauge. The temperature indicators all had warning lights; cylinder head temperatures were read from a multiple switch potentiometer, and the tower supplied the outside temperature and field pressure information.

Pratt & Whitney consulted with us during construction of the new cell, and as soon as it was operational they sat in on repeated engine tests and analyzed the final readings. They liked what they saw.

We had built the most advanced test cell in the world, so successful that P&W converted their own factory cells and Curtiss-Wright soon followed suit. Before this, we could only run in an engine on a test cell. Now we could use the cell to test an engine to the outside limits of its performance, and for the first time detect a malfunction before final test. Throughout the industry, the engine failure rate began to drop as potential problems showed up before, not when, something serious occurred in the air. The development of that cable test cell proved to be a major contribution to aircraft safety.

CHAPTER 6

# Amelia

I FIRST MET AMELIA EARHART when I serviced her Vega for a Bendix Trophy race. Our second meeting came toward the end of 1934. Paul Mantz called me at home and asked me to come over to talk about a special job. Arriving at his United Services office in Burbank, I was surprised to find Amelia waiting with him. She was not given to much small talk, so without preliminary discussion she asked if I would service the Pratt & Whitney Wasp engine on her latest Vega, adding that she had been impressed with the work I did for her at PAC.

I didn't know then that Paul's company was preparing the ship for a flight that turned out to be one of the worst-kept secrets of Amelia's career. Mechanics seldom were privy to events in which they weren't directly involved, and we didn't ask questions. These things were all in a day's work.

It was a flattering request, but I had to remind her that I was employed by Pacific Airmotive. That was no problem, she said. She'd already talked with Eddie Cooper about it, explaining that she had a big project for the Vega, and Eddie had given his permission. Checking with Eddie, I learned that the permission had been granted, albeit reluctantly, but as long as I didn't get too tired to do my work at PAC I could moonlight for Amelia. Her fame and her quiet charm made it nearly impossible for anyone to turn down a request from Amelia.

So for three or four nights a week until the job was completed, I worked on the Vega in which she became the first to fly solo between Hawaii and California in either direction. She was usually in the hangar with me, and we got on well.

In her unique fashion Amelia was quite a lady, although it is well known that she punctuated her airport conversation with a spectacular lexicon of aviation vulgarities. This was especially the case when she had trouble contacting the tower, because she was notoriously lazy about learning to use the radio properly. She would get so frustrated that her language became unprintable and Burbank tower operators often found it necessary to reprimand her. That failure to learn radio procedures may be significant in light of the apparently frantic transmissions before she disappeared. I remember Paul Mantz telling her that she must be up to speed on frequencies for daylight and night transmissions, but she flippantly replied that if she couldn't get what she wanted she'd just keep trying until she got a response.

The mechanics at PAC liked Amelia because she treated everybody as equals; whenever you were working on her plane she was right there, watching but never interfering. And Amelia never failed to let you know when she was pleased with your work.

I have a particularly vivid recollection of one of her spontaneous expressions of appreciation. Paul Mantz had set up a special job on her Vega at PAC, but neither he nor Amelia told me that she was afraid of its engine. When I finished servicing it, she took the plane up on a test flight, and on landing she jumped out of the pit, threw her arms around me, and gave me a kiss that forever will be burned into my memory. She said the engine had been so rough that it shuddered in flight, but now it was smooth as glass and she didn't have to worry about it any more. If that kiss was an indication of her gratitude, she was so grateful I didn't think I would tell my wife about it. Amelia could be very unsettling around men, especially young mechanics fifteen years her junior.

I next worked with Amelia in 1936 after she acquired the Lockheed Electra for her attempt to be the first to fly around the world at the equator. As one of the cooperating sponsors, Pratt & Whitney supplied the Wasp Junior engines and asked Amelia to bring the plane to PAC for testing and outfitting. Polly and I both got to know her at this time because Amelia often insisted on taking us out to dinner when Polly called for me during a late working night.

After the Electra was made ready at Pacific Airmotive—which by then had become a division of the Bendix Corporation—Amelia flew the plane to Oakland and spent a few days installing the long-range fuel tanks she would need on the flight. Then, with Paul Mantz as co-pilot, Paul Manning as navigator, and Fred Noonan as backup navigator, she took off for the first leg of the trip, Mantz at the controls because of the extra-heavy load of fuel.

They flew to Hawaii without incident. From there she was to continue with only Captain Manning and Noonan as navigators. It is commonly reported that Amelia ground looped on take-off from Luke Field in Honolulu. Something certainly did happen, but there are inconsistencies in every account I have read. My own conclusions may be controversial, but they are based on three pieces of evidence: what I was told by a Bendix Aviation technician who observed what happened; the physical evidence I saw when the plane was returned to Burbank; and private conversations with Amelia in the aftermath of what truly was a mystifying occurrence. Nobody but Amelia, and possibly Manning and Noonan, really knew.

The damaged Electra was packed up and shipped back to California on one of the Matson liners. Many days before it arrived at Burbank more or less in pieces, I heard a first-hand account of the incident. The Bendix man, who had been sent to Honolulu to help Amelia with any problems that might arise with equipment Bendix had supplied—brakes, magnetos, generators—had called Eddie Cooper from Honolulu to tell him about the accident and report that the right brake had been burned. He returned to Burbank about a week after the accident. After talking to Eddie he found me in the hangar on an engine work stand and waved me to come down so we could talk.

"Art, when the bird arrives, please look her over real close and tell me what you think. I was over half-way down the runway when the accident happened. She had her tail high, and I thought she was about to lift off when she ground looped.

"I was first to get to the plane. The brakes were our responsibility, so I borrowed some tools from a Navy truck and removed them. The right brake was badly burned and the left was absolutely normal. I heard only one engine reduce power.

"You know Amelia is one damn fine pilot, and how she could have this accident is beyond belief. All we could get out of her was that she just didn't know how it happened. Something's fishy!"

Accident investigation was fairly routine for me by then, as I had inspected several mail plane crashes for the Department of Commerce. Although I heard and vividly remember everything he said, it didn't hit me immediately that this man was speculating that Amelia aborted the flight with a deliberately faked ground loop that was supposed to look like an accident.

It did seem strange to some of us at Burbank. When news of the accident reached the mainland we had discussed how in the world she could ground loop at almost flying speed. As pilots of tail-dragger aircraft know to their eternal chagrin, a ground loop can easily occur during a crosswind landing when the plane is going too slowly for good rudder control. It turns itself around.

I once ground looped and remember the force that put me to the side of the pit, which meant the plane was swinging out with more force than the gear would permit, so the outside gear doubled inboard.

It's important to mention here that I was never told the direction in which she had ground looped, so naturally I assumed that Amelia had burned her *right* brake trying to correct a fast high-speed *left* ground loop, normal procedure with an accidental ground loop.

The bird arrived in boxes at PAC, where we were to disassemble the wreck and disperse the parts for repair. At Amelia's request, I was put in charge of the crew, and got two big surprises when we opened the boxes and saw the condition of the plane as we began to lay it out on the floor.

The right wing and the right gear had suffered all the damage, as was expected for a left ground loop, but the right gear was collapsed *outboard*. In a normal accidental ground loop to the left, when the right brake was scorched, the right gear would have collapsed inboard. (Contrary to some reports, the gear was not torn completely away.) The second surprise was the state of the propellers, which already had been removed. The blades on the right prop were bent forward, indicating a high-powered contact with the ground. The left prop blades were straight and only slightly scuffed where they had touched the ground.

A much later surprise was to read an erroneous report that she had blown a tire. Both were fully inflated and on their gear when I first saw them. The wheels had to be removed in order to remove the brakes, but it would not have made sense to change the tire before reinstalling the wheels.

I said to Amelia, "What's going on here? This couldn't have been a normal ground loop. It was forced. Why?"

Very calmly she told me not to mention it and to mind my own business. So I told her that we had better do something about the gear. She asked me why. I reminded her that the inspector was to arrive the next day to make an official accident report, and that he'd know the gear and brake condition never would have been caused by an accident.

"Damn! I forgot about the gear," she said. "Art, you and I are good friends. You didn't see a thing. We'll just force the gear back over to make it look natural. Will you promise me never to say anything about what you know?"

I said, "Sure, Amelia," and I kept that promise for fifty years.

After the crew had gone home I jacked the wing up off the floor and with an eight-foot pry bar Amelia and I forced the right gear over center to an inboard position. The main support had been torn loose, so it wasn't difficult. As we worked, Amelia told me that in Honolulu she was in the plane and ready to go when she received information that somehow she must abort the flight. She did not say why, who issued the order, or how it was delivered. Unfortunately for posterity I didn't have sense enough to ask, but I don't think she'd have told me. Nor did she directly admit to deliberately faking a ground loop.

Yet the evidence then, and now, was clear to me. My analysis is that she decided to abort by faking a last-minute ground loop on take-off, but forgot to consider her high speed and the extra weight of the fully loaded aircraft. She applied the right brake to accelerate the ground loop but because of the speed and weight she burned it. Then she tried to slow down the action by applying all the power she had on the right engine to correct too much looping; *or*, knowing she was going to the right, she may have simply reduced the power on the left engine. Either way, it was no accident.

There have been reports that the aircraft ended up to the left. This could have been possible considering that Amelia was trying to correct for an intentional high-speed ground loop to the right that had gotten out of hand.

The Bendix tech rep had gone back East by that time, but I remembered his last words to me. "Take a good look at the damaged gear. We have the brakes over at Bendix. I haven't said anything about it—just turned them in without a written report. But I don't think it was an accident." Tech reps have to be careful about expressing opinions, and to my knowledge he never did talk about his suspicions.

I also remember hearing Paul Mantz, who had given Amelia countless hours of instruction on the Electra, raising hell with her because that aircraft couldn't possibly ground loop at take-off speed. Her only response was, "Get off my back about it!" We thought that was strange, too. It's no secret that Paul and Amelia were very close. Apparently she hadn't told even her most trusted advisor what she really did.

Several other theories have been advanced about the cause of the accident. The two most frequently stated are that she was jockeying the throttles in direct contradiction to Mantz's instructions, or that she cracked up the Electra accidentally because she was incompetent to handle it. But I am not alone in the belief that she was ordered to abort the take-off (which she actually told me) and did it the only way she knew how.

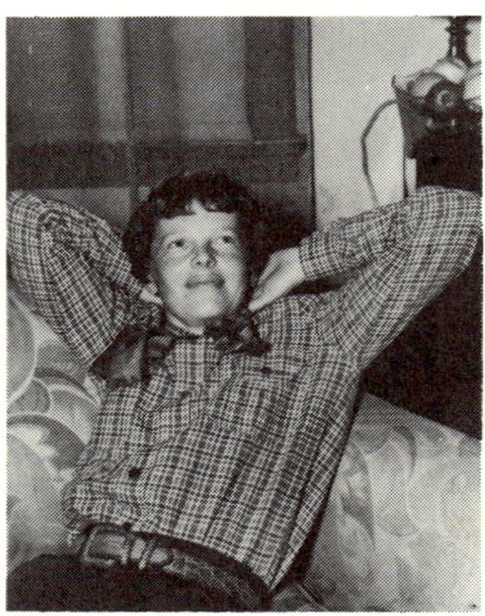

*Amelia Earhart as sketched by the author (left) in 1937, and in a rarely seen photo in Oakland, c. 1936. Photographer Carl Bigelow of the* San Francisco Chronicle *was a good friend and volunteer publicist for Walter Varney.*

The night we bent the gear back, Amelia took Polly and me to dinner, but she seemed nervous and said that a lot depended on my keeping quiet about what I'd seen because she was going on a special mission that had to look like a routine attempt to go around the world. She said, "Can you imagine me being a spy?" then she sort of tittered and added "I never said that!" Polly later was to volunteer an account of this evening with Amelia when she was present during hangar flying bouts with close friends.

Although Amelia had a house at Toluca Lake, she did not have a car and didn't like to go home alone late at night. So she frequently stayed at the Del Monte Hotel in Burbank, down the street from the Pullman restaurant where we had just eaten. On this particular night we dropped her at the hotel. Amelia gave me a big hug and said, "Remember, we are friends and friends are faithful." Then she gave me another faithful-friends kiss and slipped a fifty dollar bill into my hand. Polly and I were shocked. It was more than half my monthly salary.

Next morning Jimmy Reed, the Department of Commerce aviation division inspector, arrived to make the official accident investigation. Paul Mantz and Todd Oviatt were with him as witnesses. He looked at the plane closely, and when he got to the wheel well he stopped and drilled right through me with his eyes. "Art, were you working on this plane last night?"

As casually as possible I told him I'd only cleaned out the mud and sand the gear picked up when it went off the runway hard pan. Jimmy said to Amelia, "I'm really ashamed of you, such a good pilot letting a plane get away from you, especially on take-off!" but he was looking at me. Amelia gave me a big wink.

Jimmy finished the inspection, then walked me to the hangar doors, which had been closed to keep visitors and the press out. He and I were old friends.

"I owed you one, Art," he said, and walked off with "you know you're a lousy liar!" I never found out what he saw that convinced him I had messed with the gear, but he was very sharp, and it could have been the way some of the sheet metal was torn. Regardless, he kept his suspicions to himself, perhaps because once I had done him an important personal favor that had nothing to do with aviation. I was relieved that he hadn't seen the props, which I'd already taken to the shop, or the brakes, which Bendix had. As it was, I felt guilty. It was the only time in my career that I intentionally covered up accident results.

We removed both engines for our shop to repair, then loaded the fuselage and wings onto a lowboy trailer to be driven over to Lockheed. A couple of weeks later a Lockheed friend showed up with two company engineers and asked to speak to me privately. "Art," said my friend, "I've known you a long time and I know you're an honest man. Tell us the truth now, because it means a lot to these fellows and what they do in the future. I promise it will go no further. Now, did you or did you not mess with the original position of the gear on A.E.'s Electra?"

I was annoyed at being put on the spot. "Yes," I answered. "So what?"

"Don't get your dander up, Art. That's all we wanted to know." One of the engineers said, "Well, that settles that. We do *not* have a rudder control problem," and they left.

Soon after that, PAC got a rush order from Lockheed to make two-inch adapters for the generator pad of two Pratt & Whitney R-1340 engines. They told us they had made the mount, but discovered there wasn't enough clearance for a new type of heavy-duty generator they wanted to install as an experiment.

Our machinist made the adapters and drives and I took them to Lockheed to see if they would fit. Carl Leipelt, who was in charge of engine buildup at Lockheed, and his supervisor, Firman Grey, worked with me. This was one of the first Dynafocal installations with shock absorbers in the mount. No one was sure of the range of the engine's movement through torque.

The engine was in the mount and it was impossible to make the adapters pass through the mount ring. I had to hand-file a one-inch radius curve on the forward side of the adapter and relieve the bottom half to pass the ring.

The trial-and-fit process took quite a while. As we finished, I glanced down at the bench and saw the work order for the job I had just completed. It bore the serial number N16020. That was Amelia's plane! But her Electra had Wasp R-985s, which my company was in the process of overhauling for Pratt & Whitney.

I asked Carl what was going on. He got very flustered, picked up the order so I couldn't read any more of it, and said it was "from the front office" and they had made a mistake on the number. But he pleaded with me not to say anything or he could lose his job. I promptly put it out of my mind. At Pacific Airmotive we continued to overhaul the original Juniors, which we tested and sent to Lockheed to install.

When I went over to do a final run-up and check on the oil screens, I noticed that they had installed larger fuel tanks than were there before.

After Amelia was lost I recalled the incident at Lockheed. Stories were coming out that the Navy was looking for her around the Marshall Islands. I realized then that the original R-985s never could have gotten her off the tropical field at Lae, New Guinea, with the fuel load of 1,200 gallons, which was much more than she needed for the last leg of 2556 miles to Howland Island. I have seen a copy of a letter from Lockheed's Robert Gross to George Putnam detailing the weights and possible ranges of the Electra "as is" with the Wasps. The 1,100 gallons of fuel she took on in Lae, plus what probably was in the tank, far exceeded the gross take-off load indicated in the letter.

One piece of the puzzle fell into place during the war when I was an inspector at Lockheed. Carl Leipelt, Firman Grey, and I were hangar flying one day, and I asked him about the adapters we had worked on. Firman acknowledged that he and a crew had taken the two R-1340s to Indonesia and installed them on Amelia's plane there. Carl said he was aboard for one of the trial fuel consumption runs of more than 1000 miles. With 600 horses in each of those larger engines, the bird had gotten a heavier load off the ground, although the speed was not greatly improved in long-range, low-power cruise condition. Firman firmly told me that information was not to go any farther. The record indicates that Amelia stayed in Bandoeng, Java, for six days. This supports my theory that Amelia was not planning a direct route flight. Otherwise she would not have needed the extra fuel and the larger engines to take off with the heavier fuel load.

There has been much speculation about the engines on Amelia's bird. According to files in the Smithsonian Institution's National Air and Space Museum, the Earhart Electra was a model 10E approved, under Type Certificate No. 590, to be powered by two Pratt & Whitney S3H1 engines. The license application filed with the Department of Commerce, Bureau of Air Commerce, on November 27, 1936, and the restricted license subsequently issued to the aircraft, dated to expire August 19, 1937, further state that these S3H1 engines were built to specification number 143 with a rating of 550 h.p. per engine.

This seems to indicate that Amelia's Electra was delivered with the Wasp engines. However, she flew the first test flight with Elmer C. McLeod on July 22, 1936, and was in the Bendix air race from New York to Los Angeles on September 4, 1936. Jane's first listing of a 10E, incidentally, is in 1937. It is possible that the license application filed in November of 1936 was in anticipation of changing the engines at a later date.

In any case, the engines we removed after the Honolulu crash and that we later overhauled were Wasp Juniors. I tuned up these engines after they were installed on Amelia's bird at Lockheed prior to her departure. It is possible that they could have been changed any time thereafter, of course, but I believe that Firman was telling the truth.

Sometime in the mid-sixties a newspaper published a picture of an engine fished out of a bay either in the Marshall Islands or Saipan—I'm not sure which—thought to be from Amelia's plane. The Marshalls are far northwest of Howland, where she was supposed to have been headed. The photo was clear enough for me to recognize what appeared to be the special adapters I fitted on Lockheed's R-1340s. I remember showing the photo to several friends and writing to Eddie Cooper about it. It lends some credence to those, including myself, who speculate that Amelia went down near Mili in the Marshalls. Considerable evidence exists that she and probably the Electra were picked up there and taken to Saipan by the Japanese.

This was some time after Paul Mantz produced a generator supposedly found near Saipan, which he said the Japanese told him was from her plane. Paul gave the generator to Eddie Cooper, who personally delivered it to the main Bendix factory. Upon disassembly it was found to be a perfect Japanese copy of the generator on Amelia's plane except that, unlike hers, the bolts had metric threads.

Now that half a century has passed it seems appropriate to record what I know. Most of the people still alive who knew Amelia refuse to accept the so-called "spy theory" of her last flight because it simply did not fit with her character. I would have been among them had it not been for what she told me about the aborted take-off in Hawaii. It has been suggested also that I was dazzled by Amelia's charm and well-known reluctance to take the blame for any kind of accident, even to the point of lying to me to cover up her incompetence at the controls of the Electra in Honolulu. However, the sequence of her remarks to me would have had to be a masterpiece of deceit if she were trying to cover for mere incompetence. If she ever told anyone else, undoubtedly she exacted the same promise she did from me. Unfortunately, I cannot call on any witness to verify the account. Only Polly could have confirmed what Amelia said to us at dinner.

I do not believe that Amelia was a spy in the usual sense of the word. I do believe, however, that someone in the intelligence business recognized, almost too late, that Amelia's flight offered an unusual opportunity for the Navy to take aerial photographs of the Japanese installations in the South Pacific. To do so, Amelia would have to fly from West to East on a long overwater flight, "miss" her scheduled destination, and land on some remote island. In an apparent search for her the Navy could take their photographs and then "find" her. This plan would work only if a way could be found to abort the East to West flight and if the "legs," or range, of her aircraft could be increased. Alternate destinations, even for a crash landing, are few and far between in the South Pacific. I think that Amelia's "spy mission" was simply to provide an excuse for the Navy to do their spying.

Speculation and theories aside, however, I can attest to Amelia's real passion for making that flight successfully. Away from the pressure-cooker promotion that George Putnam always created around her, without having to keep up appearances for high-powered famous friends, she was relaxed when she was with Polly and me. After all, I was just her mechanic. Still, we had our love of aviation in common, and Amelia confided that if she pulled off this flight she would be so famous that the aviation industry would be *obliged* to give her a good job. I asked what she had in mind.

"For one thing, I want to prove myself to the airlines as a qualified pilot. And I want to get involved in developing and testing aircraft in a large factory." Coming from a woman who already was one of the most famous personalities in the world, her wish struck me as wistful, almost childlike. However, I didn't move in her circles, and only recently have come to realize what a dedicated feminist Amelia was.

Amelia Earhart was not a saint; she once told me frankly that she used men to further her flying career. Undoubtedly there were better woman pilots among her contemporaries, especially those whom

George Putnam considered enough of a threat to try, usually successfully, to keep in Amelia's shadow. Nevertheless I believe Amelia worked at developing her piloting skills and toward the end became one of the best.

Certainly there is some truth to the contention that Amelia was the creation of the public relations expert to whom she was married. For me, though, she remains a remarkable and courageous woman who earned her unique niche in American history with a rare combination of charm, spunk, guts, and luck.

The last time I worked with Amelia was when Pacific Airmotive sent me to Lockheed to give a final run-up on the engines we overhauled following the Honolulu accident. Amelia and Firman Grey were with me in the cockpit. Firman left after we finished the run-up, but Amelia hung back for a moment. She said, "Art, please don't forget our little secret," and climbed out. I never saw her again.

At the risk of introducing a note of mysticism to this account, I must relate that one night while I was writing these memoirs, I dreamed about Amelia. She looked straight at me and said, "Tell the truth." I have done that.

CHAPTER 7

# Jolly Colde England

THE SINISTER SOUNDS coming out of Europe in 1938 were echoed in military projects underway throughout the leading companies of the American aviation industry, among them Lockheed and Douglas in Southern California. Their neighbor, Pacific Airmotive, was being drawn into several of them. A reconnaisance aircraft for the British RAF eventually took me to England, but before that assignment I became involved briefly with the unique airplane whose first customer was the country that two years hence would stage a surprise attack on the United States.

Early in the year Eddie Cooper assigned me to drive the Ford pickup over to the Douglas Aircraft Company each day and check in with the Bendix and Pratt & Whitney reps. Do whatever they asked, Eddie said, and when I wasn't busy just stay out of their way. I was puzzled.

"Why me?" I asked.

"Because right now you are the only one I can trust out of my sight, and besides you have the best tools and you know how to use them."

As I turned to leave, he added "Oh, by the way. You're getting a raise, effective immediately."

At the Douglas factory, the guy at the gate seemed to know who I was and sent me out to the experimental hangar. There sat the biggest airplane I'd ever seen. It had four engines and three tails and dwarfed everything else in the hangar.

"What in hell is *that?*" I asked the Bendix rep. "That," he replied, "is the new DC-4!" It was the first—and only—three-tailed DC-4 ever built.

They asked me right away to check the valves on one of the new auxiliary power units (APUs). On this first four-engine aircraft built by Douglas, they were sure the electrical demand would be too much for the generators of that day, especially if they lost an engine. The APUs were mounted at a 45-degree angle in the number one and number four nacelles. To work on them you had to be a contortionist with three elbows and eyes on top of your head.

This early DC-4 was powered with a new P&W R-2180 twin Wasp engine. (Later one-tailed production models were powered with R-2000 engines with double clutches for high and low blower operation.) When the test flights were finished Douglas and P&W ordered complete overhauls for the R-2180s because they had a buyer waiting. The buyer was Japan, and that's where the DC-4 finally went. I helped remove the four engines and took them over to PAC in Burbank, where we disassembled, reworked, and reassembled them for running on the test cell. After final checks, they were reinstalled at the Douglas factory and I was sent back to PAC.

Two days later, Cooper called six of us into his office and asked each man in turn if he had somebody ready to replace him. Nobody did, until he got to me, at which point I told him of a mechanic I had trained and felt was ready to do my work.

"Art, how would you like a foreign assignment in England for Lockheed?" Eddie asked. It didn't require a second thought. "Hell, yes!"

When I got home and told Polly, her reaction was just as quick, even if I had accepted without consulting her first. Her only complaint was that it would be two months before we could leave.

I must not have been too dumb, at twenty-five. For a long time I had been convinced that the growth of aviation was outstripping the supply of good mechanics. Wherever I was, I'd pick out a likely candidate and start him on a training program.

Pushing my people upward never hurt my own career, as I first discovered with the assignment to England and later was to prove over and over again.

Reporting to Lockheed for training, I learned that the British Air Ministry had ordered 250 B-14s to use as general reconnaisance aircraft. At a cost of twenty-five million dollars, this was the largest order ever recorded by an American aircraft company.

Basically the B-14 was an Electra with a larger fuselage and Wright G-105 engines that developed 800 h.p. on takeoff. The British christened it the *Hudson* in deference to the Air Defense Command's penchant for names rather than numbers, in this case to commemorate the explorer Henry Hudson. I was to work at Lockheed's reassembly division near Liverpool, staying with the airplanes from the time they arrived in England by ship from New York, and teaching servicing and run-ups to the British mechanics.

The first B-14 was scheduled for delivery to England sometime in February of 1939. Just after Christmas, Lockheed told eight of us technicians and our wives to be ready to leave Burbank by train on January 5. Their people met us in New York with tickets and instructions to report to the Cunard liner *Aquitania* the following day.

Once aboard and standing in line for table sittings, we were pleased to find that our good friend Henry Ogden was also on his way to England for Lockheed. Hank and aviation were synonymous in those days. As a seventeen-year-old Army recruit from a small Mississippi town, in 1924 Hank had won a berth on the U.S. Army's famous round-the-world flight of three specially equipped Douglas DT-2s. Among other things, that flight marked the first crossing of the Pacific Ocean in any aircraft and inspired Douglas' famous trademark of three airplanes circling the globe.

When he returned to civilian life, Hank designed and built a trimotor airplane from scratch and called it the *Ogden Osprey*. He powered it with three Menasco Pirate engines that delivered a good 125 h.p. The bird flew so well on these with a pilot and six passengers that it could maintain 5000 feet on two engines. Hank was way ahead of his time.

Once he joined us aboard ship, Hank didn't waste any time asking if he could room and board with Polly and me in England, since he was the only single man in the Lockheed group and didn't want to live alone. He was more than welcome in our home; Hank stayed with us until Lockheed promoted him to take over the reassembly division in Liverpool.

At that point his British colleagues announced that his living in the home of a "lowly mechanic" was unseemly, so he had to move out. We continued the forbidden friendship by meeting in a pub for dinner, or he would sneak out to our house for a game of pinochle. This was not our first, nor would it be our last, encounter with the rigors of the British class system.

Hank was responsible for the success of Lockheed's wartime assembly plants in England, Ireland, and Scotland. After the war he returned to Burbank and became a vice president in the Lockheed training program.

The Atlantic crossing was uneventful except for some excellent partying, thanks to the presence of a clutch of celebrities including the Mills Brothers, who descended from their first-class quarters to entertain the cabin-class Lockheed group with songs they never would have dared sing even in nightclubs. We landed at Southampton and went by train to London, where the company had made reservations for us at the Strand Palace Hotel. Unaware that private baths were not abundant in London hotels, we were dismayed when the hotel management assigned us to shabby rooms with no bathrooms, forcing us to run up a flight of stairs and down a long hall to use the head. This inconvenience was intensified by one of England's coldest winters, which made the prospect of a hot bath very appealing.

A sign over the bathtub directed guests to call the chambermaid to make an appointment for a bath. I did this on our second night there, making arrangements for a "very hot bath" at 9 P.M., to which the maid responded that I was to "knock her up at nine." She did not take kindly to my answer that I would have to get my wife's permission.

Promptly at nine I called and asked if the bath was ready.

"Aye, sir, that it is," she said. "I made it a bit full, you know." I put on my robe and eagerly negotiated the long voyage to the frigid bathroom. Dropping the robe, I jumped into my hot bath—and right out again. It was ice cold!

I rang for the maid.

"Didn't I ask you for a very hot bath?" I yelled through chattering teeth.

"Oh aye, sir. I drew it very hot for you before I went to tea," she replied in an injured tone.

"And what time did you go for your bloody tea?"

"Oh, about six o'clock this eve, why?"

I reached over and pulled the drain plug.

"Oh, sir! You can't do that. The water has to do for three more clients!"

That did it. I roared back to the room and called the manager, who took umbrage at my accusation that the hotel had no hot water for its guests. They *always* turned the furnace off at 7 P.M., and why hadn't I called the chambermaid? I told him what happened. "You Yanks are a bit queer, you know," he observed. "We have no complaints from our other clients."

"That's because the dirty Britishers don't know what a proper bath is, by the smell of them!" I retorted, and he hung up on me.

It nearly caused an international incident. The hotel summoned the Lockheed representative, who was in the midst of scolding me for being rude when Hank Ogden and the other three couples appeared and said they would be going home unless something was done about our quarters. Before long we were moved to luxurious suites with private bath at the top of the hotel and plied with flowers, Pinch Bottle Scotch, and profuse apologies.

It seems a clerk had thought we were "only" technicians and mechanics and not deserving of anything better than the cheapest rooms. When my behavior was reported to the foreign office, they informed the hotel that we were guests of the King. And so we were treated for the rest of our stay in London.

In Liverpool, we were assigned temporarily to the Adelphi Hotel, where, thankfully, we found private bathrooms and extra blankets to keep us clean and warm while we looked for housing near Speke Aerodrome, located about fifteen miles southeast of Liverpool on the Mersey River. The search turned up some government housing and we were installed in the two-family duplexes the RAF was building at nearby Hunts Cross. Not what we were used to, but we quickly adapted to the rather more Spartan lifestyle, made the place comfortable with some of our own amenities, and settled in for eighteen months or 250 B-14s, whichever came first.

Since the airplanes hadn't yet arrived, the Lockheed people started to work on the hangar assigned to the B-14s. We anticipated as many needs as possible, building stock rooms and shelves, partitioning off the hangar from the shops, enlarging the bathrooms, and requisition-

*Left to right: Walter Varney, Anne Johnson, Polly Kennedy, and Art Kennedy photographed at the Hofbrau restaurant, Hollywood, California, 1938.*

*Polly Kennedy at Hunts Cross, England, 1939.*

*Henry "Hank" Ogden doing homework at Art and Polly Kennedy's quarters near Speke Aerodrome in Hunts Cross, England, 1939.*

ing two hot-water showers. Hot water problems again! During one very trying day I tried to explain that when an American gets sweaty, he likes a hot shower. Said one bloke, "But we never shower. I take a bath when I remove my winter underwear in May!" Keeping quiet put a severe strain on my slowly developing diplomatic skills, but it was good practice.

After that got settled, I decided to go home a little early. All of us were using bicycles for transportation. The British were about to impose stringent gas rationing and everyone had advised us not to buy a car, which would be too expensive anyway. The Bristol Blenheim factory at the other end of the aerodrome employed more than 10,000 people, all released from work at the same time I started home that day and exiting directly into the roundabout at the end of the airport road.

I was still mulling over the day's challenges and forgot that the British drive on the left. Absentmindedly I entered the roundabout the wrong way, headlong into a huge mass of bikes. The resulting pileup damaged twenty other bikes, totaled mine, and inflicted severe lacerations on my arms, legs, and dignity.

When a Bobby came along to help straighten out the congestion, he took one look at the mess and began to laugh. Then everyone else started to laugh, and before long we all were doubled up and someone suggested we adjourn to the corner pub. Two hours later I staggered home with tubes and wires hanging about my head and shoulders and never did convince Polly I'd been in an accident before, not after, going to the pub.

My new friends got me another bike at a good discount and from then on, Polly and I were among the few Americans who mixed with the British. Still in our twenties, we were learning the art of making friends in other countries, good preparation for the overseas assignments we had in later years.

The Lockheed crew had nearly finished the hangar projects when we got news that the first airplanes were about to arrive on a freighter at the Liverpool docks. We all went to the boat to see how the birds had been shipped, and found that the wings were packed separately from the hulls, and the tail feathers crated with the propellers. So far not so bad.

Towing those big B-14 hulls through Liverpool's narrow streets presented a nightmarish problem, however. At first we even considered barging the planes up the river and dredging a passage into the aerodrome. Finally, the crew obtained some city maps and made several dry runs on motorcycles until they found a route wide enough to accomodate the hulls. The town fathers then decreed the towing would have to be done after midnight, which was further complicated by the necessity to raise wires that hung low over some of the streets in order to get the airplanes under them. The RAF officer in charge of our British mechanics quickly sliced that bit of red tape. One midnight shortly thereafter, five wingless B-14's were tractor-towed through the black streets of Liverpool and thence to Speke Aerodrome, where we got to work teaching the British how to maintain and fly them.

CHAPTER 8

# Sabotage at Speke Aerodrome

DESPITE ALL THE SIGNS to the contrary, way into 1939 the British man in the street evidently believed that their beloved Neville Chamberlain was going to out-talk Hitler. At the aerodrome, however, we Americans were given the distinct impression that the military was trying to tell us, without actually saying so, that the government knew war was coming and that they had very little to fight it with as far as aircraft were concerned. Activities at Speke were permeated with a sense of urgency.

As soon as the first B-14s arrived we started to assemble them, teaching the RAF technicians as we worked. Discovering that the five left wings were following on another boat and wouldn't get to Liverpool for at least fourteen days, we decided not to install the right wings until they arrived. Meanwhile, we prepared the first two birds for run-up to expedite their delivery to the RAF.

When we informed the officer in charge that we were going to run up the engines without the wings and check all systems except autopilot and flaps, he became quite agitated.

"But I say! That can't be cricket, y'know," he stormed, and the next morning we found the following astonishing notice posted under "Orders of the Day": "THIS COMMAND WILL NOT SUPPORT THE RUNNING OF ENGINES WITHOUT THE PROPELLERS BEING IN-

STALLED." This prompted some wry speculation among Lockheed personnel that he didn't know a wing from a propeller. I understand this notice stayed posted at Speke until after the war.

Needless to say, we had a good laugh, and as planned, took the aircraft out, tied her down, and blocked her well. I got into the pit and was ready to start her up when the CO flew out of his office waving his arms and yelling, "Can't you bloody Yanks read the order of the day?"

Since the aircraft belonged to Lockheed and would not be turned over to the RAF until after the test flight, I was still in charge on the ramp. I hollered out of the cockpit that we could indeed read, we were not disobeying the order since the propellers were firmly attached to the aircraft, and would run up the engines.

He got on his motorbike and tore down the field to his headquarters, returning later without a word to anybody. We never heard from him nor saw him again in the hangar or on the ramp.

The first B-14s were equipped with Cyclone 202 engines with Chandler-Holley carburetors. These carbs were bastards to start if they were extremely cold or allowed to sit for a long time, and both conditions prevailed here. However I thought I could overcome it. We already had depreserved the engines in the hangar, but I needed

*British conscript mechanics the author helped train at Speke Aerodrome, photographed with the second B-14 to arrive in England. Aside from the few indecipherable autographs, identifications are not available. Note that no turret installation is evident on this early "Hudson."*

more help than that. I told the ground crew I wanted to be sure they were clear, so they were to turn the props through by hand until they saw gas come from the gurgle tubes.

While they did this I started to prime by hand as hard as I could. When they finally shouted that gas was coming from the gurgle, I hollered "clear!," got a loud response, and hit the starter button. After one revolution, I turned on the switch and immediately heard the "pop" that said I had a start. I kept hitting the primer to keep it going, and soon we had 1000 rpms. The engine settled down to a nice, even purr and the Lockheed and British personnel gathered on the ramp signaled a collective "thumbs up." We got the same result on engine number two.

Neither our own nor the British pilots ever could get a good start with those engines until I explained my system for this peculiar carburetor to Lockheed's test pilot, Milo Burcham. He would be taking the planes to other bases to teach the RAF how to fly them, and was not anxious to have the Brits think the B-14 was a difficult bird to start.

"I'll be damned!" he said. "You know, I always use the primer but only *after* I hit the starter button. How do I persuade these blokes to pull the engines through each time?"

"That's easy, Milo," I replied. "They all know the problem of hydraulic locks in the cylinders. Their Bristol Jupiters are famous for bent connecting rods from not clearing the engines, so you tell them the same thing could happen to the Cyclone, only more so."

The left wings arrived after we had given five airplanes their first engine run-over. Wings installed, the first aircraft successfully passed its final run-up and flaps autopilot check. After I signed it off, Milo decided it would be best to have two people aboard for the test flight. As the only Lockheed technician there with flying experience, I was elected.

I had never flown with Milo, but I knew him, having once installed a pump and tank on the Boeing 100 he took to the Paris Air Show to win the International Acrobatic Competition. Milo's grand finale was to perform, with smoke going all the time, a complete four-point hesitation roll in each quadrant of a 360-degree circle, ending up in his own smoke. He also created a sensation by flying that same airplane from San Diego to Los Angeles upside down.

After only one flight with him in England, I knew why Milo Burcham to this day is considered to have been one of the world's leading test pilots. He tested everything, not once, but several times, including feathering and maneuvering on one engine. His stall and recovery procedures were a work of art. His 360 two-needle width bank and turn check against a stop watch was letter perfect. He was in absolute command.

It was while we were testing the fifth bird for delivery to the British that the first sign of trouble appeared. Everything had gone well until roll-out on take-off. I was pumping slowly but steadily on the wobble pump when the red warning light for a fuel pressure drop came on and Milo yelled, "Pump like hell! We're losing pressure on both!" I pumped like hell, but to no avail. Milo cut both engines and tromped on the brakes while I put the flaps down, and we executed a smart controlled ground loop.

Milo wanted to try it again. We ran up each engine to full power, held it, and watched, but no fuel warning light came on. Next he ran up both together with brakes on. Still no warning lights. Finally he put both engines to max with brakes on, told me to mind the wobble pump, and be ready to jump on the brakes with him if we didn't make a good take-off. We started down the field and were about to lift off when the bloody lights came on and stayed on. This time we went back to the ramp.

For a week we tried to find the trouble, installing new wobble pumps, checking all lines for flow, and rechecking the warning system. We found nothing, so we took her out again. Once more, at about lift-off, both lights came on.

By now we suspected fuel starvation. Starting at the tanks, we removed every line and fitting up to the engine. At a group of fittings just before the wobble pump tie-in, there was a junction where the two tanks came together, fed the wobble pump, and then separated. I looked into the exit and saw what looked like a piece of colored cloth. Roy Buckminster, our shop chief, was looking over my shoulder and saw the same thing.

"Don't touch it!" he commanded as I reached for it. "Remove the entire junction and don't give it to anybody else but me." Buck handed the fitting to a British civilian who had been hanging around the ramp since our first incident with the warning lights. The civilian told Buck to seal off the aircraft and instructed him, Milo, and myself to accompany him to the nearby Bristol factory.

We went directly to the test laboratory, where they told everyone but the operator to leave and sealed the doors. We hooked up the junction exactly as it was on the aircraft, with the fuel flow in the same direction from the two sources.

"Can you judge approximately how much time elapsed from the time you opened the engines until you had a fuel warning light?" he asked Milo.

"Sure," said Milo. "It was nineteen seconds until the fuel lights went on and twenty-three seconds until the first sign of a power loss."

The civilian's jaw dropped. "How can you be so sure?"

"Easy. As I reached full power I hit the stop watch on my panel and noted the time each event happened." Nothing ever escaped Milo's attention.

The operator turned on both sources and set the flow to max. We watched the rotometer on the bench for starvation. It started to drop at twenty seconds. At twenty-five seconds it dropped sharply to almost no flow.

"Well," said the civilian, "that's just what we are looking for. It agrees with the information we have."

At this point they let us in on the great mystery. "We" were the British secret service. They had been informed that one of the birds had been sabotaged during disassembly after being flown from the Lockheed factory to New York. The police were holding a suspect on a trumped-up charge, having no evidence of the sabotage, but time was running out. The secret service man rushed out to call New York, and we began careful disassembly of the junction.

Inside we found a strip of cloth about a yard long, meticulously accordion-pleated and tamped down into the elbow of the fitting. It was so expertly done that with the flow reduced it would retract and permit enough fuel to pass for normal run-up. But under pressure of a fuel flow at max rate it would creep out until it restricted the flow. When the flow dropped it would retract again until the fuel could flow once more.

It was an admirable piece of work, except that the timing was off. If it had been designed to take longer to cut off the fuel flow, we could have lost the bird and possibly our lives.

They invented a cover story for our replacing the fittings and inaugurated new testing procedures. We were sworn to silence and sent back to work on our side of the field. Back in New York, our intelligence people discovered the Nazi saboteur was a German national who had jumped ship there and somehow worked his way through clearance to get a job as a mechanic with Lockheed.

As B-14s arrived with increasing speed, England's bad weather made it necessary for Lockheed to send two more test pilots. Whenever the fog rolled in from the Mersey River the field could stay closed for days at a time, and if the sun did come out it was for only two to four days. With these frequent interruptions in flying weather, as many as ten or twelve birds would stack up and need to be tested at the same time. Our new men were Joe Towle, who stayed with Lockheed until he retired, and Frank Anderlion, an ex-Varney airline pilot.

One beautiful day Milo and I were on test with a little extra time to play. For the hell of it, Milo started a split S. On one pull-up into a half stall the bird went completely out of control and we found ourselves upside down. Milo fought her around and right side up. He was a little white, and angry. No aircraft *ever* got away from Milo.

We still had another bird to test that day, so we went home to get it. Milo intended to try the maneuver again to figure out how it had happened. I had both engines running on the other plane when Milo came out of the hangar followed by Frank Anderlion, who was putting on a chute as he came up to the pit. Milo said he had a call from the States, so Frank would take this flight and attempt to duplicate the maneuver that had gotten us into trouble. I explained the maneuver to him and Milo told me to give him some more details when we were in the air so Frank could try it.

"Okay," I said, "but man, I'm tired!" We already had flown five birds. Johnny Hagerdorn, a Lockheed inspector, had taken only two flights with Frank that day. He overheard me and said, "I'll take this flight if you want, Art."

I thanked Johnny and gave him my chute. As I left, Fred Taylor, my new mechanic, came out with a chute on. He said he had permission to go on a flight if I approved, something he'd been wanting to do for a long time. Naturally I said it was all right, and told him the best ride was in the bombardier's seat in the nose. They took off.

About an hour and a half later I was at home when Buck came running into the house with tears in his eyes, hardly able to talk.

Frank had lost a wing. The plane crashed on the other side of the river and everyone had been killed.

Milo and I rushed to the crash site. The RAF already had removed the bodies, but told us they found Fred trapped down in the nose and Johnny stuck half in and half out of the rear escape hatch, where his chute had caught.

Frank's overhead escape hatch was missing. He could have gotten out but apparently rode the broken bird down, waiting for his crew to get out first.

The right wing and the right stabilizer and rudder were gone. Everything else seemed normal. They found the wing twenty miles down the road, loaded it on a lorry, and brought it back to the wreck. When we laid it out in about the right position, Milo said, "Does this look natural to you fellows?"

It certainly didn't. The flaps on both wings were more than six inches out. We checked what was left of the cockpit and found the flap handle in "down" position, which it should not have been under normal flying conditions.

We packed up the wreck and sent it back to Lockheed for further investigation. Three months later the official report came back from the factory. At the time, flap handles on the B-14 were simple up-and-down devices with no locks. Lockheed's entirely plausible explanation for the accident was that the bird had been in some kind of violent maneuver that caught Johnny by surprise in the co-pilot seat. As he felt the ship go, he probably grabbed the flap handle rather than the wheel to steady himself, inadvertently pushing it down. The additional load with the flaps down put too many Gs on the wing; it failed and fell off, clipping the tail feathers as it left the bird, which apparently maple-leafed down and hit flat.

Lockheed sent us some new mechanisms with instructions for installing trigger-type locks on the flap handle so it could not be operated without first pressing the lock. These were installed on all Lockheed aircraft from then on.

If Milo tried that stall maneuver again, he never did it with me aboard. He may have experimented when he took some of the planes aloft by himself after test flight, because he warned everyone who flew the B-14 that under certain conditions it was inclined to have a high speed stall with no warning, and told them how to recover.

It was a tragically narrow escape for us and a terrible loss of our friends. But we had to keep testing, and by now Milo and I were such a good team that he announced to Lockheed he would not make test flights with anyone but me. We didn't know there was another interesting experience in store for us.

For that matter, neither did anybody else, which is why Hank Ogden called Milo and me to the Adelphi Hotel in Liverpool for a confidential meeting with Clarence L. "Kelly" Johnson. Kelly already was a renowned designer for Lockheed, and would become even more famous for the Lockheed "Skunk Works," where he directed the secret development of highly advanced aircraft.

During supper Kelly casually announced that the new turret had been delivered and was being readied for testing. Milo and I were assigned to do it.

"*What* turret?" asked Milo. "We don't know anything about a new turret!"

Kelly always was unflappable. "Oh, that's right. You wouldn't know. The British have built a top-secret hydraulically operated gun turret for the B-14. We don't have anything like it in the U.S. We've been adapting the Hudson for it, and if it works, they'll put it in all their bombers."

Milo was dumbfounded. "How are we supposed to test this thing?"

Kelly explained that the turret was not symmetrical and would need to be turned continuously during high-speed tests and vertical dive runs to be sure the cam system worked so the gunner wouldn't shoot off the tail feathers. The British were at that very moment installing the prototype on a B-14 at the Wolverhampton factory and would be finished tomorrow.

"We want you to check for buffeting, and then use live ammunition while operating the lift cams to verify interruption as they pass the rudders and stabilizer tips."

"Well!" I said. "I see I'm nominated to operate the turret as well as ensure the aircraft is okay for service, with a chance of blowing off our tail and trying to get out of this bloody contraption. Is that right?"

"That's about it," said Hank. "You have a right to refuse, but we'll have a hard time persuading Milo to take anybody else with him."

"You're goddamn right, Hank," replied Milo. "I can tell you right now that without Art you get yourself another pilot."

*Clarence L. "Kelly" Johnson, famed designer-engineer with U-2 he developed at Lockheed's secret "Skunk Works."*

They were in a spot. I wondered just how tight it was.

"Hank, you know I've been doing test flights since the first birds arrived, which is above and beyond my ramp rat duties and being responsible for safety before testing. All this time I've been getting regular mechanic's pay, and I don't think it's right."

Kelly got the message and quickly authorized Hank to pay me co-pilot's overseas pay on test flights and all benefits and expenses while we were at Wolverhampton.

Over $175 a month more! I could hardly refuse.

Next morning we were on a train bound for the Boulton-Paul factory in Wolverhampton, where they were building the Defiant fighter. Sporting its new turret, our B-14 stood in a corner of the ramp, surrounded by a high curtain and armed guards. We climbed aboard and Kelly spent the first day instructing me on the complicated cam interrupting system that automatically lifted the twin 30-caliber guns when they came in line with the rudders and stabilizers. That night in the hotel, we went over the system again, Kelly asking questions and correcting my answers if they weren't precise.

The RAF already had put quite a few hours on the B-14. Milo began to distrust their maintenance and insisted that I shake it down for safety. An officer testily reminded us they had done a complete inspection themselves, and besides, they were in a great hurry for the turret test.

"The bird will be inspected by my man or you test the turret yourselves," said Milo. The officer unhappily conceded, and I asked him to assign three mechanics to remove the cowling and open inspection doors to speed the operation. At the end of the day I presented Milo and the RAF with more than a hundred discrepancies to be worked off before the plane could fly.

Kelly asked for a copy of the list. He was disturbed, because the British had not had the B-14 very long. If the list was a reflection of their maintenance practice he wanted the head office to know about it. Lockheed's reputation was at stake.

While we were trying to figure out how long it was going to take, the RAF sent in a contingent of technicians headed by a man on loan from one of the major airlines. His military authority derived from a hastily conferred tunic and the honorary title of Wing Commander. Even though it was obvious *he* didn't think much of us Yanks, either, we liked him at once. Because of his expertise, David Montrose probably was going to be a friend, and we needed all we could get.

The still-grouchy RAF officer handed Montrose a copy of the list and asked him to determine which repairs he felt were essential and how long it would take to make them. He spent the day going over it and that night asked for a conference with Milo, the RAF man, and myself. Milo and I were afraid we were facing another battle, but we had agreed not to back down on a single item.

Montrose announced that he had gone over everything on the list and couldn't imagine why anybody who claimed to know aircraft would even think to dispute it. Then, to our embarrassment, he gave the RAF officer a tongue lashing that concluded with the news that he was going to report to the High Command about the deplorable condition of a B-14 in such a short time since delivery.

So the RAF started to work, and Milo and I wondered how we were going to spend the next ten days in Wolverhampton while they fixed the airplane. It wasn't too long before we found out.

CHAPTER 9

# Fixing Things at Boulton-Paul

THE NEXT MORNING Milo and I were paged in the hotel lobby by a distinguished looking gentleman who introduced himself as the general manager of the Boulton-Paul airplane factory, and could he have a word with us? Having nothing better to do, we followed him into the parlor.

It seemed he had been discussing me with David Montrose and heard from others that I was experienced in production. I don't know where they got that impression. Until then my only production experience had been on motors at Pacific Airmotive in Burbank, although I had done a lot of organizing in various shops.

Neither of us denied it, however, and before we knew it, Milo and I were being taken on a grand tour of the Boulton-Paul factory with a view to soliciting our advice on how to improve production of the Defiant. At the end of the tour they sat us down in the front office and began to ask questions. Milo said he was a pilot and knew nothing about production and they should address their questions to me. All heads turned. I had to stall, so I said it was an impressive place, but I'd need at least three days to become acquainted with their system before I could give any intelligent answers.

They had already obtained Hank Ogden's approval for us to spend the free days at the factory while we waited for the Brits to make the

B-14 flyable. That settled, the front office gentlemen said in unison, "Fine, we start in the morning."

That "we" made me uneasy. "I hope that when you say 'we,' you mean just Milo and myself. I don't want anyone looking over my shoulder."

"Look, old chap," said the manager, "we can't do that. We're making a secret machine here. You must be accompanied."

Milo stepped in. "But, sir, we're all allies with the same objective. I understand your War Office is quite perturbed about your lack of production. I'm sure they will give us clearance to do our investigation alone and turn in a proper report."

They agreed to the clearance. On the way back to the hotel I asked Milo, "Where the hell did you get the idea they're in trouble?" The Boulton-Paul executives certainly hadn't admitted it.

"Right up here," he said, pointing to his head. "Why would they ask for help from a damn Yank if they weren't in trouble?"

Milo probably had it figured correctly. The manager was very eager for us to come to the factory, and if he promised clearance overnight he must have had it already. It had taken *us* three days to get clearance to visit the Bristol plant at Speke.

Next day we were warmly welcomed and handed badges that permitted us to enter any part of the factory. It was also admitted that the War Department had given the plant notice about a month ago that they were to deliver at least one Defiant a day and to be prepared for an increase in the demand. So far they had been able to cut only half a day off a dismal production schedule.

Before long the reasons for their deficiencies became abundantly clear. Their most obvious problem was filth. Second only to that was the lack of light. I had never seen a factory so poorly lighted. Men working under the wings couldn't see to do anything correctly, always dropping something that took a long time to find in the dark and dirt.

The third major problem was tea time. What seemed like hundreds of tea wagons pushed by girls in dirty white uniforms roamed the factory with urns of strong hot tea, sugar, milk, and biscuits. Because so many workers couldn't afford the ha'penny for tea, they would try to cadge freebies from the girls. The time lost in wheedling and drinking tea was astronomical.

From the final line we went to the sub-assembly section and found the same problem, except it was even dirtier, the floor littered with rivets, bolts, nuts, and other things we couldn't identify. In this garbage pit they were trying to attach bare wings to the hull, too many people clustered around the bird to see what they were working on.

In the fabrication department we found still more filth and wasted manpower. One big group was cutting up sheets of aluminum into smaller sheets, which went to another group marking designs of pieces to be cut out, and then on to individual cutters.

The stockroom aisles were lighted only by pale low-wattage bulbs every ten yards or so. As we walked along we were hit by an odor so foul that we guessed the whole factory was using the dark corners for an outhouse.

By now we had a flashlight. Milo was talking to me and walking backward when he turned into a blind aisle and bumped his fanny against something. He turned the beam on it and there was a girl's foot waving in the air. She was on the floor, with some bloke screwing the hell out of her. Scrambling and cursing, they got up and ran toward us, trying to escape. Scrambling just as hard to let them out, Milo and I succeeded only in getting in their way. Then Milo pointed the light farther down the aisle. What appeared to be about twenty more couples, in all states of dress and undress, got to their feet and rushed past us.

We got to laughing so hard that we had to go to the men's head. Another shock. It was nothing more than a long trough, a running-over open sewer. The stench made us sick to our stomachs. The six wash basins also were overflowing and stinking. We quickly backed out and went to the front office to use the white collar workers' head, which wasn't much better.

It was more than enough for one day. We returned to the hotel to prepare our joint report. Milo was upset. Clearly the British couldn't win the war trying to build airplanes in a factory like the one we had just seen.

Notified that the report was ready, the manager hurried to the hotel and we locked ourselves in a conference room. He confided that he had been sent to Boulton-Paul by the War Department only a month before, and knew nothing about airplanes or production. He was supposed to find out why production was so bad and make the changes necessary to bring it into line with the urgent need for fighter planes.

"As you are aware," he said to us, "this is another of our ballups. I assure you I'll accept any advice you can offer. I'm tired of hearing that things can't be done!"

I warned him it was going to be embarrassing. First of all, I told him, an aircraft is a high-precision machine and not only is filth detrimental to its construction, but men and women cannot be expected to do their best working in a pile of shit. Next I went to the lights and suggested that the combination of cleaning up and better lighting alone should improve production.

He listened without comment until I got to the half-hour tea breaks three or four times a day, and suggested that the man hours lost in one week would allow the manufacture of one complete airplane.

"My Gawd, old chap, what can we do about that?" he exclaimed. "Tea is an English tradition. We'd have a bloody mutiny on our hands!" I pointed out that not only would they lose their tradition but all of England if they didn't shape up. They could adopt American-style fifteen-minute tea and smoke breaks before and after lunch, and the company should provide the tea.

Improving the sub-assembly line area, I told him, should involve a sub-sub-assembly line to make wings and center sections complete with ailerons, flaps, gear, armament, and lights, before mating to the hull. That way fewer people would be doing the final hookup and testing. I suggested bench assemblies for the hull, making the complete instrument panel and building the complete engine before putting it on the bird. This, of course, would require engineering revisions, but he nodded in agreement.

When we got to the stock room, I explained the importance of bright lights to help the stock clerks, and added that it might discourage the use of blind aisles for a bordello.

That got his attention. He literally blanched. When Milo told him of our experience, he exploded. "Oh no! Not in my factory! The lights go in immediately!"

The final item of discussion was the condition of the heads, leading the manager to observe that it probably accounted for the high absenteeism due to sickness.

He wasted no time. A stenographer was called in to type up five copies of the report. He instructed his production chief to set the entire night shift to cleaning up the factory and to call a conference of the engineering and production staff that night as soon as he returned. Contractors were to start installing new lights in the morning, and if the union balked they were to be reminded that this was a war effort and anybody who interfered with the improvements would be charged with treason. The manager then left the hotel to take "a wee nap" before the evening meeting, and that was that.

A few days later, he invited us to tour his factory again. A miracle had taken place. The floors were spotless and the entire plant well lighted. He led us to the sub-assembly sections, where they were setting up new lines for wings and center sections. We visited the infamous stock room. It was clean, freshly painted, and brightly lighted. There wouldn't be any more hanky panky in those aisles! The heads had been enlarged and crates of new urinals, toilets, and big round sinks were lined up ready to be installed.

As we walked back to the production office, I asked the manager what had happened to all the tea wagons.

"I was hoping you'd notice that," he laughed. "They're kept in our new kitchen and they can't roll out until the tea break whistle blows." There had been a little problem with the union at first, but they were happy as soon as the factory "conceded" the company would pay for the tea.

The production chief showed us the man-hour curve for the last six months up to this day, and the current delivery schedule. The curve was erratic until the last seven days, and then it began to smooth out, taking about a 20 percent drop every twenty-four hours. It was hard to believe, but they had rechecked the figures several times and it was true. Furthermore, the aircraft scheduled for delivery three days hence actually had been accepted by the Royal Air Force that morning, with only one reflight instead of the four to ten previously required.

Even following our recommendations could not have accounted for the dramatic improvement. What we had failed to take into consideration was the attitude of the men and women in the factory. Evidently they decided that if the company was spending so much money to improve working conditions, the country must be up against a critical situation and maybe they had better get cracking if they wanted to be part of saving it. Britain's hardy working man was about to start fighting!

Milo and I were astonished at the change. And when the front office staff, who hadn't been particularly friendly, gave three loud cheers for the Yanks, we didn't dare look at each other.

When we returned to Speke Aerodrome, the first thing Hank Ogden did was take us out to the bulletin board. Posted there was a letter addressed to Lockheed, expressing great appreciation for services performed at the Boulton-Paul factory. It was from His Majesty, the King.

CHAPTER 10

# Testing the Turret

TOWARD THE END of the time it took the RAF to work off the discrepancies on the B-14, Milo and I hung fairly closely around the bird in the company of a large contingent of British officers, who were being noticeably deferential to David Montrose.

Apparently he had carried out his threat and clobbered the maintenance high command about their treatment of the American aircraft. The officers were flyers from the bases that would have the birds and Montrose had gone to the extraordinary length, in those pre-copy machine days, of having fifty copies of the discrepancy list typed up and distributed to each of them. As ordered, they were observing, list in hand.

Montrose was a joy to watch as he worked with the young mechanics. He never scoffed at them nor scolded, patiently explaining instead why work was unsatisfactory when a man didn't do it right. He'd give him a pat on the back and tell him to do it over.

Knowing how much the flyers depended upon their ground crews and their general respect for them, we were dismayed, one day after Great Britain had declared war, when an RAF officer informed Montrose that civilians had no idea of how to handle "these bloody scum." As a flying officer in the RAF he demanded that the next offender be turned over to him to handle. "And I'll bet the bugger

*Lockheed B-14 "Hudson," first of its breed. Primarily developed for patrol and reconnaisance, "Old Boomerang" doubled in brass as dive bomber, medium-range bomber, low-level bomber, escort fighter, ambulance ship, and submarine hunter. It was chosen also as the personal plane of England's King George VI.*

won't sit for a week," he finished. Montrose said nothing, but mustered the flying personnel on the double.

"You flying chaps know I'm only a bloody civvie technician on loan to the military and I can be removed on a moment's notice. However, I'm going to tell you how to stay alive.

"Not one of you flyboys knows how to keep your aircraft operative, so you are the mercy of us 'scum,' as this man puts it. Right now you are getting a new type of aircraft you know nothing about.

"There's a manpower shortage in the aircraft industry. They are bringing in men and boys off the street and trying to make mechanics of them in only a few weeks. This officer criticizes the method I used on a man who did a little sloppy work."

He called a young conscript to step forward.

"What did you do before you were called up, son?"

"I was a printer's devil, sir."

"How much school did you have?"

"Three years, Master David."

"Did you ask to go into the Air Force?"

"Oh, no sir! They gave a bunch of us a test and shipped us off to the Felixstowe mechanics school to learn how to use tools."

"How long have you been working on airplanes by yourself?"

"Fifteen days, sir."

"Do you like your work?"

"Oh bloody yes! To be able to fix them and see them fly makes me feel fine, sir."

"Now, answer this question very carefully. Let's say you have been under pressure for many days and you're tired, and you do a little sloppy work. It is found by this officer, and he beats you on the bum until you can't sit down. What would be your reaction?"

"Sir, I have been treated as a man these last few months, especially here, and if that officer so much as laid a hand on me I would be damn sure his airplane would end up on the 'missing' reports."

Montrose turned back to the flyers and said, "Now you chaps keep what you just heard well fixed in your bloody high society minds, or your flying career will be a short one. You would be letting your country down just when she really needs you." After what seemed interminable dead silence, the C.O. quietly said, "Well done, David," and the crew applauded.

When the B-14 was ready, Montrose and I finished the inspections and he sat in the right seat, Kelly Johnson behind him, as we did the run-up and systems check. Everything was fine, so on a second run-up I let Montrose do the work. He was a natural. When we were signing off the aircraft, Dave said, "You know, I'll never make remarks about the

Yanks again, especially their technicians," adding, "When I get back to the airlines I'm going to do a lot more training than we've done before."

The B-14 now was ready for testing the innovative new turret. The British previously had produced a powered turret for their Defiant fighter, but this was the first that would permit gunners in larger aircraft to fire in any direction. It wasn't going to be much of a picnic for the gunner. The turret was small, and we had to depend on hand signals for communication. With no room for a chute, we jury-rigged a device that would let us get into one fairly quickly in case of trouble.

On the high-speed runs I was to turn the turret and stop at about every twenty-two degrees, hesitate, and feel for buffeting. At the same time I was to keep the guns going up and down and feel for vibration, and also watch that when they hit the cams they would react properly and not shoot off a vital piece of the aircraft.

After these successful high-speed runs, we tested the turret movement in a vertical dive, wide open.

During the dive I did feel some vibration and saw the rudder give a little flutter. Milo pulled out of the dive and I went up to the pit. He had felt the same flutter on his rudder pedal.

We tried it again, a little higher. Over we went, and this time the vibration was more severe and the rudder flutter more pronounced. But after repeated attempts, Milo was unable to keep her in the dive long enough for me to make a 360-degree turn with the turret. At that angle there was no way we could get the action Kelly wanted.

Finally Milo told me to strap in tight. He rolled her over on her back, pushed her into a real vertical dive, and immediately signaled me to test the turret. The moment we got to the point of vibration she gave a few sharp jerks and smoothed out in the higher speed. There were some loose bolts somewhere.

Milo was happy. By rolling over and going into a vertical the bird hit top velocity before she could get into the angle where she pulled herself out.

"Let's try that again!" Milo said. I crawled back to the doghouse while we climbed to altitude. With all the running back and forth, the heat, and the altitude, I was getting squeamish. When the signal came I gave him the thumbs up, but the minute the turret got back to "0" I signaled for bomb doors open, dropped on my belly, and heaved my guts all over the English landscape.

We had been in the air for three hours. Back on the ground everybody was anxious to hear our report, none more so than Kelly. He thought he had an answer to the vibration problem, which would involve the installation of close tolerance special bearings and bolts on all controls. Oddly enough, he was even more concerned about my getting sick. He wanted to know everything I had eaten and drunk the night before and that morning. He seemed positive it wasn't the food, but carbon monoxide from the exhaust getting in through openings in the turret and the main door.

The next day we took up a British gunner. After a couple of preliminary dives followed by one from 17,000 feet, we saw him frantically clawing his way out of the doghouse. Before I could help him out, he had vomited all over the deck. We'd forgotten to tell him about the bomb bay panel doors.

Back at the base Kelly took one look at the white-faced gunner and said, "That does it. Back to the drawing board!" He left immediately for Burbank to redesign the opening in the fuselage that was to accept the British turret, and develop a structure modification kit and instructions to forestall further carbon monoxide problems. Meanwhile we were to make some more tests, but he was adamant that I spend no more than ten minutes at a time in the turret, and at the first sign of dizziness Milo was to return to base.

In his autobiography, *More Than My Share of It,* Johnson recounted in some detail Lockheed's bidding on the reconnaissance aircraft for the British Air Ministry. The design they took to London apparently impressed the British, who nonetheless stipulated some modifications. Among the listed changes, Kelly adds ". . . and they wanted a gun turret to protect the plane from the rear and also forward firing guns. There wasn't a powered turret that would fire in any direction in the United States at that time. All these things affected the entire structure of the airplane—weight, balance, performance. This required almost a complete redesign and we decided to undertake it on the spot."

And undertake it Kelly Johnson did, redesigning the aircraft in his London hotel room with hastily gathered drafting equipment. Reading that reminded me that while Kelly was in Liverpool with us, Polly took Mrs. Johnson under her wing and did some sightseeing while we worked. One evening she came to dinner without Kelly and explained that he would be down shortly, but at the moment was testing stretch and tension with a new instrument he had just acquired. The test equipment? Mrs. Johnson's elastic garter belt, she explained with some amusement and no embarrassment at all. We all appreciated the insatiable curiosity that made Clarence L. "Kelly" Johnson a great engineer. He passed away in December 1990, after a long illness.

As the first American aircraft to enter World War II, the Lockheed "Hudson" surely distinguished itself. Among other things it pioneered transatlantic aircraft delivery, sank German submarines, tracked the Bismarck, and provided air cover at Dunkirk. Although Great Britain originally ordered our B-14 only for reconnaissance (I ran up several that had dual controls for training, however), they gained new respect for it when Milo organized an air race with a Blenheim and proved the airplane's superior maneuverability. Once at war, they began to use the Hudsons on bombing missions. On one mission Hudsons accompanied Wellington bombers and Blenheims into the Norwegian fjords to a target well protected by flak. Apparently forewarned, the Germans badly shot up the formation. Unlike the other bombers, almost all the B-14s returned to home base to earn the affectionate appellation "Old Boomerang."

The Hudson's exploits were almost legendary. One RAF pilot in a B-14 with the turret knocked off rolled over and made the vertical dive toward the water as Milo had taught him. Fifty feet from the water he pulled out and the two fighters on his tail mushed into the drink with two very satisfactory splashes.

Another B-14 reached northern Scotland with the right engine shot off and almost ready to stall. The pilot came straight in with the left engine at full power and once over the field made a fast landing and walked away from it. Still another made a landing with the crew all dead and the pilot so badly wounded that he died before they could get him to the infirmary.

After the Germans attacked Poland, we listened to Neville Chamberlain declare war on Germany on September 3, 1939. The B-14s arrived with increasing frequency. Until the U.S. began to ferry the aircraft to England, a dozen or so ships always were docked at Liverpool, each disgorging two to six airplanes at a time. In November, Lockheed wives were ordered to leave England and any technicians who wished to go home would be permitted to leave on the last boat out of the country on November 20.

Polly and I agreed it would be best for my career if I honored the contract to stay for eighteen months or the 250th B-14. She went back to California, and I was assigned to Leuchars air base in Scotland to troubleshoot some serious engine problems.

Even as the crisis deepened, what appeared to us as RAF intransigence occasionally continued to provide some amusement for the freewheeling Yanks from Lockheed. Milo and I got another dose of it when he took me up to Leuchars on a delivery flight, planning to stay a few days to brief the pilots. We were invited to have a Drambuie and then went to sign up for quarters and beds. The officer in charge assigned Milo to a private room and bath in the officers' quarters, and then said "your man can take his things out to ground crew quarters and find himself an empty bunk."

Before I could protest, Milo said, "This man is a technical representative of Lockheed Aircraft Company. He is not military and is entitled to the same kind of quarters I have."

"I'm sorry, Mr. Burcham, but he is not an officer and it's quite out of the question, y'know."

Milo poked a finger at him. "I don't give a damn about your bloody RAF rules, but if my man, as you call him, does not have quarters like mine, we'll be leaving as soon as we get the engines started."

The RAF was not persuaded. "I'm in charge here, and I'm expected to uphold this base's traditions."

"To hell with tradition," yelled Milo. "You're trying to fight a war, and if your lousy tradition prevents you from having the help of good technicians, God help you!"

"I'll do it," the officer sputtered, "but it's highly irregular."

"That won't do it," said Milo. "Give me your word as a British officer that for the duration of the war any American civilian technician assigned to this base will be given the same treatment."

Tradition didn't give in easily, but as long as I was there I was billeted in a nice room with a small fireplace and a supply of wood. They even tolerated my presence in the officers' mess.

When I went out to the line to see what could be done about problems on the B-14s, the original crews already had been moved to advanced operational bases and I had to teach the starting procedures to a bunch of green mechanics. They had been in the military for some time, figured I was a bloody civilian and a Yank, to boot, and they wouldn't listen to me. I wasn't getting anywhere with them, so I called Hank and asked to return to Liverpool where I could be doing something constructive. He told me to stay there and he'd clear up the problem. A couple of days later I was summoned to the C.O.'s office and presented with some wings, a tunic to wear them on, and an "Honorary Wing Commander" rating. From then on, all I got was "Yes, Sir!"

Working with Milo Burcham in England was a great highlight in my professional life, and I never think of his death in 1944 without a sense of deep sorrow. He was testing a P-80-A (the pre-series prototype of Lockheed's first jet fighter) that developed engine trouble near Burbank. Unable to crash land without hitting two children, he dove the aircraft into a vacant lot and perished. It was an untimely finish to his distinguished flying career.

On February 1, 1940, the 250th B-14 got to the line for test flight. That completed the contract; the original Lockheed contingent was packed and more than ready to go home.

England had been a tough assignment, yet for all the problems we felt had been caused by the unpreparedness of the aircraft industry, which was more technically advanced than ours but lacked sufficient

*Milo Burcham, Lockheed test pilot, in business suit and tie, climbs out of P-38 after a production test flight, 1941.*

production capability, and the occasional examples of elitism in the flying military, we left with a great appreciation for these indomitable Brits. Once geared up for war, they exercised superhuman determination to win it. Nobody but the British themselves will ever really know the extent of the incredible sacrifices made by, and of, their young flyers during the Battle of Britain.

The Yanks from Lockheed were proud we could be there to help.

CHAPTER 11

# The War Effort

FOR AMERICANS CAUGHT IN the chaos following Great Britain's declaration of war against Germany, getting out of England was a dicey affair. The Lockheed crew had only one way to get home, and that was on a boat out of Italy.

Four of us found an ocean tug sailing from Folkstone to Dunkirk in France. The skipper had three sons in the RAF and knew about Lockheed's work for them, so after confirming our identity he took us across the channel and refused to let us pay for the trip. He said it was his way of thanking Lockheed for their help.

Although German troops hadn't yet reached Dunkirk, their bombing raids had done a lot of damage. Stretchers full of wounded lay everywhere. All the hotel beds in the area were taken by retreating British officers, but we found a place to lay our heads when a kindly Frenchman installed us in a haystack for what turned out to be a surprisingly good night's sleep. The next morning we hiked to the broken end of the railroad line and boarded the train to Paris.

We took over one compartment, intending to keep it for ourselves. Before the train reached Calais, however, it came to a screeching halt that threw everyone onto the floor and some of the cars off the track. Something told us to get the hell out of that compartment. We dove out and hit the ground as three German JU-88s screamed down and strafed the train from one end to the other. When they were gone, the ever-resourceful French commandeered some beams and tipped the fallen cars back on the track. Hundreds of fleeing civilians climbed aboard, and we finished the trip without further incident but with lots of company in the compartment.

At the George V Hotel in Paris, as soon as the manager learned we were Lockheed technicians about to pick up a large sum of American expense money, he offered us room rates at $2.50 a day if we paid in dollars. Then four more Lockheed people arrived, having found a boat out of Brighton to Calais. Before catching the train to Italy, the eight of us visited some of Paris's best shops, where our U.S. currency earned almost embarrassing discounts from proprietors eager to abet their escape from France before the Germans took Paris. I had to buy an extra suitcase to hold the expensive lingerie and perfume I bought for Polly.

The immigration officer at the Italian border seemed to know who we were, and volunteered the useful information that the last American boat would be leaving Genoa in fifteen days. That was the good news. The bad news was that while the U.S. hadn't yet declared war on Italy, their military considered it too risky to permit us to linger in any city for more than three days. He advised us to use our two weeks seeing Italy. All of it.

We took his advice, and during a wild tour that would have put an American Express quickie to shame, managed to hit every major tourist attraction in the country. In Rome I ran into a Franciscan friar from Richmond, California, close to where I had grown up. He was homesick, so to keep me around he offered a private tour of the Vatican. I am not Roman Catholic and had not been exposed to much fine art, but decided it would be a good idea to take him up on it. Only much later, after visiting the great museums of Europe, did I fully appreciate the significance of what I had seen. Nor will I forget descending in a barn-like elevator to Vatican basements jammed with jewels and gold treasure. With poverty rampant on the streets outside the Vatican, that evidence of the church's wealth was revolting to me.

The war scare had sent most tourists home, so we were virtually the only ones around and found everyone anxious to please. At the Pompei ruins solicitous taxi drivers, predicting big tips from eight lusty Americans, made sure that we saw all the forbidden pornographic frescos, and we did not disappoint them. Our energetic sight-seeing gave us a good overview of pre-war Italy, the only disconcerting factor being that wherever we went we were tailed by a couple of sinister-looking Blackshirts, right up to the moment we finally boarded ship in Genoa.

The American liner U.S.S. *Manhattan* carried 500 passengers. All of them, except for us Lockheed technicians, were wealthy European fleeing the war, loaded with gold and jewelry. We, on the other hand, were broke, having used up all our expense money on the grand tour of Italy. Luckily, our situation did not go unnoticed by the American crew, which seemed overjoyed to see us. They gave us the best sittings in the dining room and let us run up inexhaustible bar tabs on the house. The bartender told us the ship's captain already had met our expenses by doubling fares and charging the Europeans obscenely high prices for everything.

Lockheed brought our wives to New York to meet us. The company also provided welcome vacation time and compensated us generously for the additional expenses incurred in our escape from England. So, feeling I could make a contribution to the war effort by staying with Lockheed, I went to work for them in Burbank. The United States was not yet at war, but we were helping our friends who were, and it was clear to everyone that fighters, bombers, and cargo planes were going to be needed as quickly as they could be manufactured.

Lockheed was just starting to build a mockup of the first Constellation, the C-69, and put me in charge of breakdown for the power plant and nacelles. "Breakdown" in aircraft production is the analysis and division of the operation into the several distinct processes essential to production planning. As usual, design engineers hadn't bothered to consult engine experts. Kelly Johnson listened patiently to my complaints about the impossible production designs and let us build our own mockup on the floor. Then they called for the design engineers to come down and make new drawings from the mockup. They had to throw out thousands of man hours of the original design work, but it was the only way to do it right. Among other things, the high engines on the C-69 were difficult for mechanics to access and dangerous to work on when they were running. I recommended restressing the firewall and installing a quick-fastening panel to get at the engines, with drop-down shelves for mechanics to sit on as they worked. Although it was viewed as a revolutionary idea, Lockheed incorporated it into the plans. Only twenty C-69s ever came off the line.

The factory also was having accidents on the flight line with the C-60 Lodestar, a stretch version of the B-14 Hudson bomber. They suspected it was due to faulty inspection procedures. Lockheed inspectors automatically were moved along the company seniority pipeline, but few of them had any flight experience. Since I had a valid CAA license of some years standing, they pulled me off the job I was really enjoying to take charge of inspection on the Lodestars, which were coming out at a rate of five or six a day.

I called a meeting and told the inspectors they were signing off too many C-60s. They argued, but when I directed each of them to go on the next test flight with the aircraft they'd signed off, attitudes abruptly changed. Some admitted they hadn't been thorough enough, one quit in a huff, and I quietly transferred the one who told me privately that he was frightened of flying.

Polly and I were seeing a lot of Walter Varney, who had fallen on hard times and was working as a flight line inspector at Lockheed. When I told him what I had done, Walter howled with laughter. "You bastard! You're the only one I can think of who would get away with that!" When we got into the war and production cranked up even more, Walter, always a superb pilot, flight-tested the B-17s Lockheed helped build for Boeing.

The new inspection regime slowed production for a short time, but they soon caught up to the production schedule of five or six a day. There were no more flight line accidents with that airplane.

In August of 1943 they promoted me to the production line for the P-38 fighter, which Lockheed was producing at the rate of about one and a half aircraft a day. When the Army asked for seven a day, the automobile production types then running the line told them they were crazy. Lockheed's president, Robert Gross, reassigned them and as part of the new staffing I was made a production supervisor from body mating through flight test.

The first thing we did was take the union shop steward on a grand tour to show him why we needed to get rid of thirty-two bad apples among the employees. He agreed, and within five days production had picked up by 30 percent.

We reorganized the line, introduced a parts system with stockrooms on wheels, and because the warehouse was located so far from the floor, we developed the first stock conveyor system installed in an aircraft factory. Instituting bench assembly and other new efficiencies, we soon began to supply the Army with their seven P-38s a day.

Then came Pearl Harbor. I tried to enlist in all three services, but each one told me that with my long-time CAA license I would be more valuable to the country in the aircraft industry. Well into 1942, things were going smoothly at Lockheed. I had a good assistant, and as a matter of fact, was getting a little bored. Toward the end of December, I received a letter from my friend Howard Hartman, a former Pratt & Whitney man. He was now vice president of a new company called Chandler-Evans, which manufactured carburetors and fuel pumps for military aircraft. Howard wanted me to join their field service department. With the wartime manpower freeze about to lock everyone into their jobs, if I was to make a move it was now or never. So I resigned from Lockheed and Polly and I moved to South Meriden in Connecticut.

Milt Chandler had been chief of design engineering for Stromberg Carburetors, afterward starting Chandler-Groves, which made the troublesome carburetor on the B-14. Now, with a brand-new company, he thought he wanted engineers on the field service staff but Howard persuaded him that aviation people with practical experience would be more useful. After we had been around a while he admitted Howard was right.

I traveled for Chandler-Evans for two years, troubleshooting carb and fuel pump malfunctions as the U.S. strained to meet war production schedules. One of the first assignments was in Detroit, where the Packard factory was having pressure fluctuation problems with the Rolls-Royce 1700 engine they were making for the British company, which had no production facilities in England. The Navy was worried, as this was the engine installed on their PT boats and they had to be totally reliable. It was necessary to refinish by hand the piston and cylinder cases of the dash pot while the factory carried through with the needed modifications on subsequent models. That fixed it, and the Navy stopped worrying.

The next assignment was at the Curtiss-Wright plant at Robertson Field in St. Louis. The Army was threatening to take their fuel pump business elsewhere unless something was done about problems with the C-9 twin Lycoming engines. That turned out to be nothing more than a simple matter of contamination. Chandler-Evans beefed up the cleanliness of the fuel pumps they shipped down, and the problems ceased. During all the years I worked with engines, I was amazed that so few engine people grasped the importance of cleanliness in both fabrication and maintenance.

Curtiss-Wright also had a secret project going at their Paterson, New Jersey, plant, where they were building the 2200 h.p. grandaddy of all engines, for which Chandler-Evans was supplying the carburetors. Important military airplanes—Boeing B-29s, Consolidated B-32s, and Lockheed C-69s—were sitting on production lines waiting for this new engine. When the first CPB-5800 carb was ready, they sent me to see how it worked on the R-3350 BA engine. This new Curtiss-Wright Cyclone was a monstrous thing, the largest engine ever installed on an airplane, with a complicated carburetor system requiring elaborate instrumentation. The carb had double throttles and the biggest mixing chamber I'd ever seen.

You never knew how carburetors would work on aircraft engines until they were installed and the engines run up. The crew worked all night to get the pot mounted and instrumented. Along with Curtiss-Wright's Frank Weygand and three other engineers, I went down to the test cell to witness the first start and help out if necessary.

The Army had sent a young quality control officer to observe the tests and accept the engine. I suspected he didn't know much about engines, and he proved it by announcing that he would make the first start. Frank had to tell him, in front of everyone, that the engine did not yet belong to the government, but he was welcome to do it if he would sign the DD-250 acceptance form giving the U.S. government the responsibility for any cost-plus delays he might cause. The lieutenant backed off and they started the tests.

For three hours, both the engine and carburetor performed unusually well at low rpms, but as soon as it got down to under 700 rpms, the engine would quit cold. This was carburetor trouble. I discovered that we would have to design new throttles, which Chandler-Evans speedily did and sent down two days later for me to install. Now all we needed for final acceptance was a good idle and full power run, then a satisfactory acceleration test. We got the idle taken care of, but at high speed there was too much airflow and they couldn't close the throttles.

The factory was experiencing the same trouble in their own tests. After they made a major modification in the main body of the pot and we got it installed, the operator took the engine to full power and back without further difficulty. Now for the final acceleration test.

The first time around we all thought the acceleration was just right, but the lieutenant insisted it wasn't fast enough. He wanted to try it himself. He wrapped a towel around the knob, and at 1500 rpm gave it a hell of a yank. The motor backfired like a cannon and almost quit.

Frank tried to explain that the acceleration he was looking for was suitable for fighter planes, but not necessary on a heavy bomber. The explanation fell on deaf ears. He wouldn't accept the engine.

We were in a real fix. The Army was hounding Curtiss-Wright to deliver an engine to Boeing in Seattle at once. Suddenly I got a screwy idea, which Frank thought was worth a try so they could at least get this one engine sold to the Army.

Frank put the test cell under strict security and slipped out to get a bottle of pure alcohol. We ran a line from the instrument panel to the top deck of the pot and hooked it up to a hot water bottle, which we filled with alcohol and a little water. Hiding it under a pile of rags on the floor, we put a board over the contraption and called in our lieutenant. Frank told him we had corrected the problem and invited him to try the acceleration again.

We warmed up the engine and did a complete acceptance test run, which he approved at each point. When it was time for the acceleration test, he wrapped the damn towel around the knob, set the engine at 1800 rpm, and announced that he was ready. At that juncture I stepped closer to watch him, and just as he made his move I jumped on the board. That great engine roared up and over-revved so fast that Frank had to tell them to shut it down before it was damaged. The lieutenant was delighted. He signed off the engine and the carburetor and departed, none the wiser. In three days the engine was shipped to the Boeing Aircraft Company in Seattle.

That off-the-wall stunt, believe it or not, was the first instance of water injection in an aviation engine. I got a hero's welcome at the factory. During a staff meeting Milt told me they were developing a double-capacity pump he hoped would work without the aid of a hot

*Early Boeing B-29 bomber with the 2200 h.p. "grandaddy" of engines, Curtiss-Wright R-3350 BA, fresh off the production line, Seattle, 1943.*

water bottle. He got some funny looks, but didn't enlighten anyone with an explanation.

Chandler-Evans next assigned me to the West Coast, so Polly and I moved back to Burbank. It was considered high priority work and assured us such privileges as enough gas coupons to get home and first place in line at airline counters. Along with Dick Benjamin, another Chandler-Evans engineer, I was sent up to Seattle to help work out a scoop effect bug in the Curtiss-Wright Cyclones for Boeing's new B-29. Dick and I were put on a United flight ahead of a couple of irate colonels who kept telling the girl at the counter they had to get to Seattle immediately to work on a secret bomber. A few days later they showed up at the Boeing flight line, embarrassed to discover they were assigned to assist me. But they were ready to work. We got to be good friends during the two months we spent together on the cold ramp at the old Boeing plant on the Duwamish River.

Since I was slightly senior to Benjamin, we decided that he'd be best acting as a "PR" liaison to the Boeing people while I stayed on the ramp and tried to solve the problem.

We tried all kinds of scoop-cowl combinations, looking for a proper fuel-airflow ratio to effect maximum power output with correct cooling on both ground and air runs. I had to dismantle the pot several times, and saw to it that the colonels got the job of cleaning the parts so they would become familiar with it. At night in the hotel I gave them lessons on metering and fuel control.

When the engines finally were installed on the B-29 and ready for the first taxi and high-speed runs for brake tests, Boeing's great test pilot, Eddie Allen, was at the controls. He opened the engines to full power and started down the field. But he ran out of runway and we heard all four engine shut off as the B-29 rolled into the overrun and stopped. Everyone piled out of the plane. Eddie was white. He said he had been unable to reduce the throttles on one and three and finally had to turn off the ignition switches.

It wasn't exactly the same problem, but it coincided with the situation we had encountered at the Curtiss-Wright factory, only this time it was throttle loads at take-off position instead of at low rpms. I went back to the hotel to call Milt Chandler. He said he couldn't tell me why on the phone, but I should get in touch with Boeing's chief engineer, Wellwood Beall, and tell him exactly what was wrong. That plane was supposed to fly in four days!

Beall was forced to confide to me that high officials from Washington, D.C., were coming to tour the Boeing plant and watch the first test flight of the B-29 bomber. We both realized that the only possible way they could get the plane into the air in four days was for me to modify the throttle bearing surfaces on all four carbs, while Chandler-Evans went back to the drawing board for a permanent fix.

The situation was urgent. I would have to remove the four pots, disassemble them, and "touche" all the throttle bearing surfaces and journals to obtain at least 90 percent bluing contact and a literally microscopic clearance. Each one would take several hours of hand work.

Boeing put me in a little shack, and for sixty-nine hours I worked under a machine gun-toting guard, accompanied by a nurse who poured stimulant-laced coffee into me every hour or so. I had completed three of the four when Beall came in. He asked how much longer I needed, but I was so punchy I couldn't answer. Beall said, "My friend, you've done all you can for now. Go back to the hotel, and when the nurse says you're ready you can come back and finish."

All I remember about going back to the Olympic Hotel in downtown Seattle was the nurse pouring me into bed. I woke up two days later. The B-29 hadn't flown, but Wellwood Beall had left a message with the nurse that I may have been the first aircraft technician to cause a president to delay a ceremony while writers made hurried changes in his speech. Franklin D. Roosevelt was the "high official" they'd been expecting!

The president's visit was not announced in the local papers until two weeks later, but I remember seeing a photo of President Roosevelt being driven under one of the B-29's huge engines as the plane sat on the flight line. Somebody who was there reported that his remarks seemed disjointed.

I finished the work and the B-29 made her first flight test, staying aloft for two hours. Boeing was pleased, and Chandler-Evans expressed their appreciation with a $500 bonus, considerably more than my salary of $410 a month. I was glad to return to Burbank and escape the tense atmosphere at the Boeing factory, where pressure to get the B-29 into production was hard on everyone from the company president on down.

The throttle bearing problem finally was solved in the production model, but after Boeing installed the first new Bendix low tension ignition to help the B-29 gain altitude, there appeared a slight scoop effect problem on climb. So late in February 1943, I had to go back to Seattle and try to fix it. Before I could get there, we heard about the terrible accident on February 18 when a blower fire in one engine caused the second B-29 off the production line to plow into the Frye meat packing plant at the edge of the field. Eddie Allen, the crew of eleven, and nineteen people on the ground were killed. Only after reading the news accounts of the accident did the general public learn that a new superbomber was being developed at Boeing.

Despite interminable testing of the carb on the nacelle at the factory and on the air box at Chandler-Evans, nothing worked that would satisfy either Boeing or the Army. They had no intention of slowing down the aircraft with a higher scoop, which would have been the most practical solution. Finally I designed and built a special internal metering unit that took care of the scoop effect problem completely. Paraphrasing Albert Einstein, Milt Chandler commented, "I'm glad you're not a full-fledged engineer. If you were, you'd know that what you did wouldn't work!"

This time the bonus check was for $1,500, a small fortune in those days, in lieu of the rights I had signed away in my contract with Chandler-Evans. Any invention or product improvement of my design became the property of the company and the government. The unit later was adapted for jet engine fuel control units and could have made me a rich man had I held the patent. Chandler-Evans further added to the compensation, however, by notifying the American Society of Aeronautical Engineers, of which I was not a member, that they were recognizing me as a qualified carburetion engineer making an important contribution to the war effort. The bonus was nice, but the professional recognition meant even more to me.

In 1943, two years into the U.S. involvement in World War II, Howard Hartman quietly sent word that a man from Washington, D.C. was coming to see me. When he walked into my office and introduced himself as a representative of the Reconstruction Finance Corporation, I asked, "Are you the bloke from Washington?" He laughed, but took me outside so we could talk without being overheard and "offered" a two-year contract in Brazil. Apparently I had been recommended by my friend, Charlie Bobb, manager of the E.A. Parkford Company in Los Angeles and probably the best-known aircraft dealer in the country.

It was a command performance. The United States, nervous about German dominance of aviation in Latin America, was helping Brazil to absorb the German-owned Lufthansa Condor Airlines. We were going to send down four new DC-3s and assist the Brazilians in reworking the operation and shops to American standards.

Capable American technicians were sorely needed, said the gentleman from the government, leaving no doubt that neither Chandler-Evans nor I had much of a choice. It happened so fast that within one week our furniture was in storage and Polly and I were on our way to the first of many good adventures in Latin America.

CHAPTER 12

# Flying Down to Rio

MY NEW EMPLOYER'S travel instructions, typed on onionskin paper, were fascinating. They began with an explanation of exactly where they fit in the scheme of wartime activity: The "Defense Supplies Corporation, a division of American Republics Aviation, a wholly owned subsidiary of the Reconstruction Finance Corporation, an agency of the United States Government."

Barely concealed in the bureaucratic layering was the stated wartime objective of the United States: Elimination of Axis influence over air transportation in the South American republics, and secondarily to avert the return of Axis personnel after the war. Clearly, our government was concerned that in the event of a German victory, its domination of South American commercial aviation would place the Panama Canal, among other things, in jeopardy. The instructions also emphasized the importance of our working well with Latinos, and assured us that the job undertaken in Brazil was viewed by the government as a contribution to the war effort tantamount to military service.

Polly and I went first to New York, where I reported daily to the RFC office while we ordered spare parts and tooling to take to Brazil. Except for me, all personnel were airline technicians from TWA, which had been awarded the management contract.

Before long, our office duties were interrupted by an urgent message that political considerations made it necessary to get at least one DC-3 to Brazil immediately. No sooner had we figured what to take with us and computed our load factor when another message directed us to take along two Pratt & Whitney engines waiting at Hartford, Connecticut.

The resulting new weight requirements dictated that only Dick Fagan, the head pilot, a Brazilian co-pilot, chief mechanic Donald Cook, and myself could go on the flight, along with a few tools. Polly would have to follow on a commercial flight. TWA thought my flying experience and valid A&E license would impress the Brazilians, none of us guessing the flying experience would be brought into play long before we reached Brazil.

We flew up to Hartford to pick up the engines, but found they were too big to get through a standard DC-3 door, all the airplane had in those pre-cargo-door days. The engines were trucked back to the factory for disassembly and returned in small boxes early the next morning. We spent a long and tiring day tying down loose cylinders, tucking in containers of bits and pieces, and getting the main power sections stowed.

None of us had much sleep before the dawn departure. Two hours into the flight to Miami, Fagan told the Brazilian co-pilot he was going to go back and take a nap. "Just hold this course," he said.

The Brazilian was horrified. "Mr. Fagan, when you asked me if I could handle the co-pilot's seat I agreed to it only as a maintenance man."

"Dammit, you showed me your pilot's license!"

"Oh, that! In Brazil it's my learning license for a Piper Cub. I have only fifteen solo hours."

"Do you realize we have four days of hard flying ahead of us?" Dick shouted. "Do you think I can do that all alone? We'll have to go back to New York and get a qualified pilot." He was furious.

The man almost broke into tears. He had notified his government that we were on our way and a big reception was being arranged, with the governors in attendance. Failure to appear on time would be a serious diplomatic gaff.

Don Cook could have worked the gear and flaps, but he wasn't a flyer. Dick turned to me. "I know you've had some flying experience. Get your ass in the co-pilot's seat and let's see if we can go on."

I took over. About an hour later he said, "Hell, we can do it!" and went aft for his nap.

From Miami we flew to San Juan, Puerto Rico, then via Georgetown to Paramaribo in Dutch Guiana (Surinam) to gas up for the long leg to Belém in Brazil. We were the first to fly this experimental route. Most aircraft flew to Rio via the coast. Nobody had attempted to route commercial flights via Barreiros in Brazil's interior, but in anticipation of using it Pan American had completed an airport there hoping to cut a day off their flight time to Rio. We assumed they would supply us with gas for the final hop.

When Fagan filed a flight plan in Belém the control operator there was doubtful that we could make the six-hour trip to Barreiros with 29,200 pounds aboard and not quite full of gas. He told us to try to raise the Barreiros airport at least an hour out and have them turn on the beam. If we didn't find it within twenty minutes of ETA we should change course to San Salvador. However, he added with cheerful assurance, we wouldn't have enough gas to make that, either. Convinced that we'd have to walk out of the jungle, he refused to release us until we had a two-week emergency supply of food aboard.

As we flew toward Barreiros our Brazilian ex-co-pilot related a strange account of his company losing an F-34 in the dense rain forest below. Fifteen years after the plane went down an Indian hunting in the jungle spotted a wing tip and reported it to the authorities. When they cut away the growth they found only a few whitened bones in the open cockpit, but in the cabin sat three passengers looking very much alive. Temporarily embalmed by climatic conditions and jungle growth sealing the cabin openings, the bodies collapsed when the cabin door was opened. By the time they had carried them back to civilization there was nothing left but a bag of dust and bones.

Five hours out of Belém we attempted to raise the Barreiros airport. Dead silence. We kept going, and within ten minutes of what we thought was our destination, still calling, finally got a response in English with a distinctly German accent. He said he could not stay on the air but would keep the key open for another five minutes for us to home in on. We got the bearing and realized we had been far enough off course to have missed Barreiros altogether.

The field was a large, almost perfectly round table on top of a 6000-foot mountain. Its only occupant was the German we'd talked to on the radio. He worked for Pan American and had been ordered not to turn on the beam for two or three days. He didn't know why until he heard our call and decided he must come on the air to help us in. ADF often gave false readings in that volcanic region.

He was laughing when he came out to greet us. "Don't report this to PAA," he said. "I'd get fired, for sure!

While we gassed up, Pan American's Rio office called again and ordered him to tell us there wasn't any gas and to wait for the next shipment.

"Hell, first they tell me to stay off the air so maybe you get killed, then they want me to feed you for two months until the gas comes! F—— 'em! You boys get airborne right away!" It was astonishing that even as the U.S. government was trying to help Pan Am pioneer a shorter route, they were still playing dirty when it came to perceived competition. Poetic justice, perhaps, eventually rendered the attempted new route too dangerous to be practical.

Until now, no DC-3 had taken off with 31,000 pounds of full tanks and cargo. Worse, the field was high and the ground temperature over 100 degrees F. Luckily, the last 1000 feet were downhill, after which the mountain dropped vertically into the valley.

On the round field we could line up directly into a steady fifteen knot wind. Dick took every inch he could get, held the brakes, told me to give him a little less than quarter flaps when he asked for it, and get the gear up quickly when I saw the edge of the field go by. He opened her up and we started down the field. The bird was agonizingly slow to accelerate. When Dick yelled, "Flaps!" I dropped them almost to the quarter mark. We were nearly out of runway, the wheels still on the ground. Damn! She wasn't going to fly with this load.

Fagan jerked the wheel. We bounced up, fell back hard, and bounced again into the air just at the edge of the runway. I got the gear up.

We were airborne, but she wouldn't hold altitude. Dick nosed down into the valley and eased off full power. Finally the bird leveled off and held at only 4900 feet. It took us an hour to get back to the level of the field, and another hour to climb to cruise altitude of 8000 feet.

Rio de Janeiro is one of the most beautiful cities in the world to approach by night. We came in as it was getting dark, skirting some spectacular electrical displays before finding smooth air and landing at

*Reception in Rio. The author (left) at champagne reception celebrating arrival of first DC-3 for Cruzeiro do Sul at Rio de Janeiro, 1945, after grueling flight from Connecticut. Others in photo are pilot Dick Fagan, chief pilot Correa, and airline president Bento Ribeira.*

Santos Dumont Field. We had been airborne for over seven hours, quite a feat considering the load we started out with. Exhausted, Fagan and I sat in the cockpit for several minutes before we could summon the energy to climb out of the airplane.

Any hopes of getting some rest were dashed by the cheering mob that rushed toward the DC-3, including a reception committee of government officials headed by President Vargas. Now we knew why the erstwhile co-pilot had dreaded the embarrassment of a delayed delivery flight. After what seemed endless champagne toasts, they took us to check in at the Gloria Hotel, where we slept until the next afternoon's round of cocktail parties, dinners, and more parties. It seemed like a lot of celebrating for one little DC-3.

The German airline Lufthansa Condor de Brasil, had a sizable fleet of aircraft: thirteen Junkers F-13s with cabin space for four passengers; twenty F-34s carrying six passengers and a radio operator; fifteen

JU-52s, a large tri-motor with low wings and large flaps; and two Focke-Wulf four-engine transports.

We were to integrate our four DC-3s into the airline, which had been re-christened Cruzeiro Do Sul. The DC-3s were the first American aircraft ever licensed in Brazil. In the process, we also were to de-Germanize the organization, a difficult task given the high level of competence among the German technicians, some of them second- and third-generation residents of Brazil. With the arrival of the first bird the company was ordered to dismiss all German technicians and officers and it did not take us long to realize the Brazilians couldn't manage alone. The dearth of good supervisors finally made it necessary to petition the U.S. to let us hire back some of the second-generation Germans.

A couple of weeks after we arrived, two freighters docked at Rio with spare parts and ground equipment for the DC-3s. The rest of our crew was not due for another six weeks, so I went out to the overhaul base at Ponto de Caju to unpack, store, and catalog the parts and equipment. I also showed the Brazilians how to assemble and test the two engines we had brought along, as well as update their instrumentation. It wasn't really my job, so it raised a few hackles when the TWA engine men got there.

After Polly arrived with the other wives, we moved into a nicely furnished apartment located for us by the airlines office. Still waiting for the full crew, I went to work in the stock room, helping to classify parts until our stock control man came. Working eight hours a day with a Brazilian who patiently taught me Portuguese names and numbers, I got a head start on the technical language and became fairly fluent.

Most of my two years in Rio were spent setting up production and inspection procedures and teaching the Brazilians how to keep things clean. I also helped build and organize a Q.E.C. (quick engine change) shop, and reworked some of their worn-out machines.

No new parts were coming from Germany, of course, so it wasn't long before cannibalization caught up with us and we ran out of engines for the JU-52s and Focke-Wulfs. We decided to try to adapt the Pratt & Whitney 1340 to these aircraft, because with only four DC-3s on hand it was imperative to keep the German planes flying.

Washington was notified of our problem. Shortly thereafter a U.S.

Navy baby flattop steamed into Rio with eighteen SNJs aboard, ostensibly in "strike" (military for "deep six operation") condition. Actually they were junk fuselages fitted with the new engines, props, and accessories we could modify.

The first we knew about it was notification that we were to go aboard and strip out the needed parts. Afterward, watching the flattop sail away, we could see great plumes of white spray as sailors shoved the SNJ carcasses over the stern. Had they been asked about it the Navy would have claimed the whole thing never happened.

Our conversion actually produced better airplanes than we started out with. The new center of gravity meant improved cargo carrying capacity, and the engines had much more power for take-off than the old BMWs. The props were better on take-off and more economical to operate in cruise condition. It was hard even to overload the birds.

One of the interesting developments coming out of our work in Brazil involved the JU-52s flying into the interior, where the very few open meadows were impossible for landing during the rainy season. This left many settlements without airlift availability for two or three months at a time. Then we learned that a small operation in Pennsylvania had devised a system for picking up packages with a pickup line strung between two high poles. Working with their experts, we installed a trap door and a winch system in the JU and tried it out on both parcels and people. Fortunately for the human cargo, we experimented first with goats, killing three of them before the method was fine-tuned. After that, pilots were able to pluck both cargo and people from remote jungle areas with the ingenious device. The system adapted to personnel never would have been permitted in the U.S., but in backwoods Brazil then you could do anything if it helped out residents of the interior.

By early 1945 the converted airline was well Americanized. TWA had completed their contract in Brazil, so with another good job offer waiting, Polly and I returned to Washington, D.C., and more government service in an entirely different direction.

CHAPTER 13

# Sell 'Em or Smash 'Em

WORLD WAR II ALL BUT OVER, the War Assets Administration needed a qualified man to visit U.S. air bases and determine how surplus aircraft were to be disposed of. Some would be transferred to a civilian base for sale to the public; surplus tactical aircraft either would be stored or cannibalized for accessories and put on the surplus market; the rest were to be mashed up and sold for scrap metal.

They offered good pay, transportation, a generous expense account, and permission for Polly to travel with me. After the experience in Brazil I knew I was totally unsuited to corporate bureaucracy and thought this would be an interesting job. With Polly's enthusiastic concurrence I accepted.

First came two weeks in Washington inspecting reports from the field, mostly from Civil Service people who barely knew one end of an airplane from the other. The reports were of little use except to confirm the government's need for an experienced evaluator. That done, a government pilot named Dick Stapleton was supposed to fly us to Kansas City, where I would pick up a car and drive to Vernon, Texas. Our transportation was a twin engine Cessna with Jacobs engines, also called UC-64. We were hardly airborne before we knew why it had been nicknamed the "Useless 64" and the "Bamboo Bomber." At cruising altitude less than an hour out of D.C., we began to smell smoke. Stapleton asked if I could fly. "Yeah, a little," I said, and he turned the aircraft over to me while he climbed all over the airplane, even pulling out upholstery, trying to find where it was coming from. When wisps of smoke began creeping into the cabin, he decided to land very quickly, fortunate to be right over a short runway called Highball Valley in Virginia. At approach altitude Dick asked for flaps. I hit the button and nothing happened. The electrical was out on the flap motor. While we were trying to get them down manually, at half flaps the handle broke off. Nothing to do but go for it. I hit the gear switch as we turned final and Dick sweetly touched her down within fifty feet of the start of the runway.

The smoke was coming from a rag some doughhead had left on top of the battery, so hot it burst into flames when Dick threw it out on the ground. In addition, the fuse for the flap motor was missing.

We replaced that and took off again. An hour out of Wichita one motor started to act up. The left mag was dead, but the right switch was holding so we kept going. On final over Wichita I hit the gear button and then the flaps. No green lights on the gear. On visual sighting it seemed to be down, so we took a chance and went on in. It didn't feel right, but at least it was solid. As we taxied to the hangar a guy came out and said, "Hey, did you know your gear isn't all the way down?" Nor was it locked, of course. Damned lucky that Cessna had worm gear drive or we would have been on our belly.

Dick told the hangar man to put the plane on jacks and perform a complete inspection. When the mechanic opened her up he was so appalled by what he found that he didn't think we'd believe a written list and called us back to the hangar to see for ourselves.

The worm gear was clogged with congealed black gook that we took to be preservation grease. Both mags and the breaker assembly were packed solid with the same stuff, as were the distributor cap and points on the battery ignition. We'll never know why that engine kept running.

Dick hit the ceiling. According to the log books signed off in Washington, the aircraft was supposed to have been depreserved and serviced. He told the mechanic not to make any repairs, but to take pictures and arrange for a CAA inspector to come out. As it happened, that gentleman was the mechanic's brother-in-law, a conscientious official who was on the scene within five minutes of a phone call. After inspection he came up with three pages of problems and the announcement that it would take at least eight days to render the Cessna airworthy.

Later we heard that the mechanic who had signed off the log had accepted bribes to do the same thing on three other planes. He was fined heavily, removed to a place where he could never get his hands on another airplane, and his license permanently suspended. Polly and I finished the trek to Texas on an overcrowded train.

In Vernon I inspected some UC-64s and two C-47s, the Army's version of the DC-3, forever to be referred to as "Gooney Birds" by military pilots and subsequent enthusiasts. They were put into airworthy condition and flown to Georgia for public sale. We went next to Lubbock, where literally miles of tactical birds were lined up and preserved. I approved fifty-six AT-6s for repair and flight to Georgia, but about twenty-five were so far gone they had to be scrapped. Then on to San Antonio, where several AT-11s (Beechcraft twins) were in good enough condition to be flown out.

Georgia got some L-6s (Stinson liaison observation planes) and five C-46s from San Angelo, and we moved on to Muskogee, Oklahoma, where I found twenty practically new L-6s. They had been caught outside on the ramp in hail that must have been as big as baseballs. Every one of them was riddled with big holes and in some cases the fabric hung in shreds from the wings. Washington quickly sold them in "as is" condition for $500 apiece.

At this airfield all the rolling stock assembled in front of the hangars promptly at noon, where the drivers ate their lunches without getting off the machine. I was puzzled by such conscientious behavior until I learned that they were German prisoners of war who liked their driving assignments so much they refused to leave the vehicle in case some other POW would steal it. They were so happy they didn't even try to escape. Even those lent to farmers for agricultural work had only one guard, and that was for cosmetic purposes. When the POWs didn't show for work on a farm one day, the commanding officer calmly assured everyone they'd be back. The Germans returned at dusk, apologizing for getting lost. Two prisoners who did attempt an escape came back and gave themselves up, exhausted after running for five days without ever getting out of Oklahoma.

My next stop was a lake near Muskogee, where the Army had three L-6s on pontoons, good enough to put gears on and fly out. An old flying sergeant asked if I'd like to take one up alone. I'd already made a fair water landing with him along, but this time the lake was glassy and hung with a mist like a ground fog. I leveled off on final, lost my horizon, made a perfect approach and landed fifty feet too high. She dropped like a rock and hit the lake hard enough to split the pontoons and drive the struts clean into the cabin. I opened the throttle to keep her on step and drove up the ramp, where the sergeant was waiting for me, laughing like hell.

"We've done that a few times, too," he said. "I'll just log that I was the pilot and you strike it." I did, but with quite a guilty conscience.

There was no end to the surprises in Oklahoma. At the Navy base in Clinton, the eager young C.O. there said, "Boy, am I glad to see you!" He had sixty SNJs on his lot and wanted to get rid of them right now. I told him they were saleable aircraft and if at all possible I was to authorize minor repairs and have them flown out.

"You won't want these," he assured me. "They need major repairs."

"Maybe they do," I told him, "but I still have to inspect them."

I climbed around the mess for two hours and had to agree he was right. It was a sea of corrosion, broken wings, bent gears, and wrinkled fuselages. I called Washington for authorization to scrap that many SNJs, and when I got it the C.O. shoved the scrap order under my nose and said, "So sign it right now!" No sooner had I signed the order than he led me to the window and commanded, "Now, watch!" He waved his handkerchief and there was the damnedest big explosion I've ever witnessed. When the smoke and dust settled there wasn't an SNJ in sight, just rubble, with three bulldozers moving in to clean it up.

"You mean you let me climb all over that stuff and all the time it was dynamited?" I shouted. "You could have killed me!"

He laughed. "They were well secured or I wouldn't have let you near them. I have one of the best maintenance chiefs in the Navy. When he told me the planes all were in strike condition, I took a chance. And I won!" I predicted a great future for him when he returned to civilian life.

Moving on to Oklahoma City, I reported to Tinker Field. A sergeant guarding the gate refused to admit me onto the field until I persuaded him to call his commanding officer, who I knew was expecting me. As I entered his office, Emmett "Rosy" O'Donnell leapt from behind the desk and bellowed, "I knew there couldn't be another Art Kennedy in the aviation business. How the hell are you?" Rosy and I had barnstormed together at the Oakland airport back in the twenties. This was a far tamer command than he'd experienced in Hawaii at the time of Pearl Harbor, when he had to lead a squadron of nine B-17s to the Philippines. Rosy's exploits helped write the early history of the heroic, but hopelessly outnumbered, Nineteenth Bombardment Group in the Pacific Theater.

He had only one C-47, but it was in prime condition. After inspection and runup, I signed it off to fly to Georgia, and the following day got orders to report to Kansas City for reassignment. The War Assets Administration was putting me in charge of the aircraft marked for disposition or sale to the public at Bush Field in Georgia.

Dick Stapleton was waiting to fly us there in our friend the Useless 64. It had taken three weeks to fix her, and now she was back on duty and flying well. However our trip together was delayed again, this time for a much happier reason, VJ Day, 1945. Kansas City celebrated so strenuously that it took us three days to get to the airport!

Never in my life had I seen so many airplanes in one place as there were at Bush Field. Dozens and dozens of B-24s, B-26s, P-51s, P-38s, Hellcats, Bobcats, wooden Fairchilds, AT-9s, AT-6s, C-46s, C-45s, B-25s, SNJs, and hundreds of Gooney Birds.

One of my jobs was to make certain that all fly-aways were airworthy enough for a flight to the new owner's base. We sold 567 C-47s, the new and the war weary, including some that had been shot up flying the Hump in Burma.

I also helped prospective buyers select the best aircraft for their purposes. This was important, because most of them were veterans who wanted C-47s to start up small airlines or cargo routes. They may have been good flyers, but few of them knew a good airplane from a bad one.

Sadly, not many of these eager entrepreneurs were destined to survive in business. They had enough money to buy the bird, but not enough to acquire the necessary spare parts and engines. Sooner or later, most fell by the wayside.

Smart buyers snapped up C-46s for $5,000 each and stored them in case they were certified for commercial use later on. First they had to modify the cable system, which had been jury rigged during the war as a quick and dirty fix for getting flaps down evenly. They also had to redesign the elevator tab. Eventually the C-46s were certified and the buyers who had hung on to them for almost a year made a killing.

Although at first I didn't see how we could sell all those Gooney Birds, Washington finally had to send us more. New ones with only ferry time from the factory to Bush were sold for $25,000; older birds fetched $20,000. No matter how much repair was required, we disposed of every Goon that came on the field.

Late one afternoon, about dusk, the tower reported that a fleet of C-47s towing Waco gliders was calling in for clearance and instructions. What an incredible sight—twenty-four Gooney Birds, each towing three gliders, in formation! Since it was getting dark, they made only one pass before releasing the gliders, seventy-two of them hitting two runways all at once. It was chaos. Some missed the airstrip and slid into the hay field, one hit the river, and the others piled up on the runways so fast that two landed on top of the B-24s.

We scattered to help the injured and clear the runway for the C-47s, which had to land in the dark. One of them overshot, piled into the fence, and washed out a brand-new Goon parked nearby. Miraculously, injuries were confined to broken limbs and one head injury.

By now we were selling aircraft so fast it was difficult to keep up with the ferry flights; nevertheless on some days we managed to release as many as twenty-five birds. The non-saleable aircraft were dismantled by a contractor, who took out the engines, landing gears, tires, brakes, props, instruments, radios, and seats that might be interchangeable with equipment on saleable aircraft. The hulks were torn apart by Caterpillar tractors, pounded into aluminum cubes, and shipped out for reclamation. We found a different use for the wooden Fairchilds, which made grand bonfires for our Bush Field beer busts.

Some of the buyers made a lot of money from our surplus equipment, and often I helped them do it. When we had a sale of 200 PD-12-1 carburetors in their original boxes for $1.50 apiece if you bought the lot, I persuaded a Florida friend to buy them. Later, I suggested he pick up sixty-six Pratt & Whitney R-1830-86s new in the original boxes for $125 apiece. The magnetos alone were worth

$500. Not long after that, I talked him into buying the passenger seats from twenty C-54s for $50 apiece and before he could get them home a major airline bought them for $175.

As a government employee I did not benefit from those sales, but it was the start of a fortune for my Florida friend. My only extra income came from an occasional overtime final inspection for buyers in a hurry to get home.

What I liked best about this job was the opportunity to help make some dreams come true. Jess Hart, my old friend from Varney Airlines days, showed up one day to buy an airplane as a Christmas present for his son. Jess had his heart set on a P-51, which the kid had flown during the war. I picked out a bird fresh from the factory and put him in the cockpit. He sat there for a while, then climbed out with a long face and said, "This is great, but I'm sure I can't afford a brand-new one."

"Sure you can," I told him. "I'll bet you the best dinner in town that you can afford it."

"Knowing you, I've already lost the bet," Jess laughed. "What's the pitch?"

"Can you cough up $500?"

"Come on, Art, quit pulling my leg!"

I took him into the office, where my supervisor pulled out a bill of sale, signed it, and handed it to Jess. All fighter aircraft, regardless of condition, were selling for the same price. Jess peeled $500 from the $10,000 bankroll he had brought along and paid for the P-51 without looking at another bird. Who was pulling whose leg!

Jess asked to make the test flight. He went off to the far end of the 10,000-foot runway, slowly opened the throttle, kept the tail down, and lifted off. Up went the gear. He pointed the bird to the heavens and was out of sight.

We waited and waited for him to come back. Suddenly we could hear him, but there wasn't a sign of the plane until somebody pointed down the field. There he was on the deck, everything open including the toolbox and coming for the administration building at more than 600 mph. He slow-rolled her in a climbout, came back over the tower upside down and rolled out into a vertical climb, which he followed with a superb landing.

Jess climbed out of the pit a happy man. "Now I know why my son is so crazy about P-51s!" he grinned. I have been told that the son, whom I never met, became a Continental Airlines captain like his father was, and spent his spare time working on or flying his Christmas present.

The devotion of some of our clients to their aircraft was wondrous to behold. Three men who served together in the war bought a dog of a Gooney Bird that needed lots of work before I could release it. With practically no money to spend on repairs, they moved into the airplane, sleeping in it and eating out of cans.

First they had to re-cover the elevator. They went into town, bought some sheets and (we suspected it was by a midnight requisition) got a bucket of dope, needles and thread, and eight cord for the rib stitching. No pinked tape was available, so they cut strips of sheeting and with plain scissors tediously pinked the edges. It was a good job and easily passed inspection.

The bird also needed new instruments. I authorized them to scavenge some from a B-24 the contractor hadn't gotten to, and they found a good autopilot in a C-60 waiting to be scrapped. All in all, they made a good airplane out of a wreck. I signed them off and they flew home happy as hell. When I last heard of them, they were doing very well carrying fresh fruit from Florida to New Jersey.

CHAPTER 14

# The Latin Connection

HOWEVER GREAT THE COST, World War II propelled commercial aviation into a brand-new era. Not only did it accelerate the development of more efficient aircraft, but hundreds of young pilots emerged from the service well trained and eager for a flying career. And as the public acquired a new appreciation for air travel, airlines proliferated in the most unlikely places.

A good aircraft technician could write his own ticket to almost anywhere he wanted to go, and by now Polly and I, our interest whetted by the experience in England, wanted nothing more than to see the rest of the world. After about a year at Bush Field I accepted an offer from a Miami operator named Connie Shelton to go to San José in Costa Rica and help a small airline called Transportes Aeros Nacionales integrate a couple of Gooney Birds into their little fleet of three Avro Ansons. We flew one Goon down, taking Polly with us. Connie returned to Miami, leaving me to reorganize the family operation.

"Papa" Guerra, as he was always called, managed the airline; his daughter Teresa was the bookkeeper; the son, Pieque, was the excellent chief pilot. He had to be good to fly in Costa Rica. "Mama" Guerra was a great beauty, but she terrorized the family by helping herself to money from the company till whenever she wished and refusing to account for it. My first move was to buy a new till with only two keys. I kept one and gave the other to Teresa. Her mother threw a good Latin tantrum, but to the delight of the rest of the family—and immense benefit of the airline—Mama's domination ceased.

My next lesson in Latin intrigue was inspired by the loss of one of the Avro Ansons, a loss TAN could ill afford. When a built-up wooden spar was irreparably cracked during a landing, the insurance company weaseled out of paying the perfectly legitimate claim. Not long after, the plane burned to the ground under mysterious circumstances and the insurance company had to pay off. TAN now could buy Gooney Bird number two.

It seemed necessary to use any ingenuity at hand to solve problems, chief among them the Costa Rican airfields, which were unpaved, tight, and dangerous. These conditions had the single positive effect of keeping the pilots alert but the acrobatics required to get in and out of those fields was hard on engines. I never could figure out how TAN's airplanes stood up as well as they did.

One hair-raiser was the old field at Puerto Limón, a sloping beach little more than 3500 feet long, with both ends obstructed by large stands of 100-foot palm trees. By skillful landing on one wheel and taking off on hard-packed sand close to the water, the Avro Ansons could use the field, but even a lightly loaded Gooney Bird couldn't make it. Because the palm groves were on government park land, nobody had been able to persuade park officials to remove a single tree.

One night at a party I was discussing the problem with the agricultural attaché from our embassy.

"I gather you'd like to get rid of some trees, eh?" he said. "Copper kills them, you know."

"How do you put copper on a guarded park tree?" I asked.

"Use your head, man. Target practice with copper-nosed .22 bullets!"

It was worth a try. From then on, every time a crew flew into Puerto Limón they got out their .22s, invited the unsuspecting park rangers to join the fun, and plunked away at the offending palm trees. A different target each time. Three months later a high wind knocked down the judiciously selected targets. Nobody ever investigated, and eventually there was an excellent low approach and take-off clearing.

TAN was now doing a good job flying the freight, which up to then had been buried in office bins and getting to the airfield only by

*Unloading TAN's new DC-3 at a jungle stop in Costa Rica, 1947.*

chance. Conditions were primitive, but we reorganized the procedures, labeling separate freight bins with the destinations, and the family began to use them properly. The clients stopped complaining. Never mind that they might pick up their freight with an oxcart backed up to the airplane door, or that Pieque usually needed to announce his arrival by flying low over the village and buzzing cattle off the field before he could land.

The little airline became the talk of Central America when the Guerras began to run the extremely profitable La Vuela de Las Putas to United Fruit's banana plantation headquarters at Parrita. The four-hour trip by train or car was accomplished by the Goons in only eighteen minutes. Every Friday afternoon they stripped out the benches, installed a carpet, and loaded the plane with forty-seven petite Tica whores. They paid $5 a head for a round trip, the company making $235 for thirty-six minutes of flying. It was so popular they were booked up four weeks in advance, and some of the girls took to scalping tickets for double the price.

After we got TAN running smoothly, Bob Forestblade, an ex-TACA pilot, came as a permanent replacement and I returned to Miami and the job Connie Shelton was holding for me. Connie had a number of interesting projects underway. One of them was the conversion of a surplus PBY Catalina into a luxurious airplane for Madame Chiang Kai-shek.

We began by removing the flight engineer's station from the wing pylon and putting the controls in the cockpit, where the aircraft would be operated by a two-man crew. In the now-empty pylon they installed a shower, then built a round bar in the bubble area, which provided a sensational view for passengers sipping cocktails en route. Aft, five luxury bunks were built in and curtained off with fine Chinese silk furnished, of course, by Madame Chiang. The furnishings also included two large divans, an easy chair, and a small kitchen. It was a very plush airplane for those days.

I hadn't minded working for Connie, who was a nice guy when I was on my own, but working with him hanging around the shop wasn't so good and I was becoming unhappy on the job. This was the situation when Polly and I ran into Dick Mitchell, our old friend from Air Ferries days in Oakland, at a Miami restaurant. Dick was managing a commercial repair and overhaul facility in Miami and asked if I'd

*Anson Johnson with the P-51 that established a world speed record after modification at Aircraft Service Corporation, Miami, Florida, 1948.*

come and run his engine shop. I gave Connie my notice and spent the next year and a half at Aircraft Service Corporation.

We never lacked for interesting work, but the engine jobs were much more intriguing than the glamour projects, such as refurbishing a C-47 for Arthur Godfrey. One day a flyer named Anson Johnson walked into my shop unannounced and asked if we would tackle the job of overhauling and converting a Rolls-Royce Mark 3 engine. He had just bought a late model P-51 at Bush Field and wanted to install a Hamilton Standard propeller on it to enter the international air races. He had done some research and was sure that with a little reworking the Allison nose section could be made to fit that prop.

It took weeks of hard work and head-scratching, but we did it, and when Anson took it out and opened her up over the ocean he exceeded 600 miles an hour, a world's record. At the races he broke the world's speed record by 23 mph. The guys in our shop were ecstatic, and Anson left a case of Jack Daniels at my house with a note thanking us for "the smoothest engine ever."

Anson then took the bird to the Cleveland Air Races and easily won there, as well. He reported that he was so far ahead of his closest competitor, Cook Cleveland in his famous F-4G Corsair, that he throttled back to about three-quarters power to save the engine.

There was an amusing aftermath, however, when the committee examined his plane. One of the technicians made a fuss about the Hamilton Standard prop on the Rolls-Royce engine. He questioned Johnson, who only shrugged and said, "I dunno. I just turned the plane over to Aircraft Service and told them what I wanted."

The committee chairman phoned me and asked how a standard spline prop could be installed on an involuted splined engine. It hadn't been at all easy to accomplish, so I told him that it was quite complicated but if he'd send me a check for $2,000 I'd be glad to forward a set of blue prints. They decided it wasn't worth arguing about and gave the prize money to Johnson, anyway. He came home a hero, laughing about my bluff but kind enough to share $2,000 of the prize money with me.

In 1949 Aircraft Service got a contract to convert a surplus C-54 to a deluxe airliner for Avianca, the national airline of Colombia. Felipe Moniño, Avianca's director of maintenance, accompanied the aircraft to Miami, where we worked together and became quite friendly. I had

*Work ramp at Avianca, Barranquilla, Colombia, 1950s. Test cells and DC-3s in foreground, three-tailed L749 Constellation and DC-4 behind. Adjacency to dense jungle required extraordinary precautions. An employee was lost, another shot a nine-foot black panther. Snakes abounded; one young python was captured, named Elsa, and installed in the parts stockroom to control troublesome bats until she outgrew the shelf space and was returned to the jungle.*

a lot to do with the preliminary design, as well as choosing the lightweight material that made the C-54 lighter than the other birds they had in operation. Moniño seemed impressed. On delivery day he offered me a job in Barranquilla, Colombia, as power plant engineer and technical advisor to their engine and accessory overhaul shops.

Avianca found a way around Colombian labor laws to offer 35 percent more than I was presently making, furnished housing, and two round trips a year to Miami. The single stipulation was that I was not to divulge the arrangement to anyone, most particularly a Colombian. The salary, in fact, was higher than the president's.

One reason I accepted was my growing anxiety about Polly, who had begun to show signs of severe mental strain. Unable to diagnose the cause, her doctor suggested that a radical change of scene would be good therapy, which proved to be the case. Dick Mitchell was familiar with the situation and insisted that I take the Colombian job. Polly responded well to the idea, enthusiastically set about preparing for the move, and we flew to Colombia together.

In Barranquilla we were met at the airport by Dale Smythe, an American aeronautical engineer acting as maintenance supervisor and Moniño's assistant. "Smitty" quickly outlined Avianca's current troubles.

The airline's international routes were in jeopardy. Engine problems, accessory failures, and the resulting delays plagued every long trip and sometimes even the Bogotá-Barranquilla run with DC-4s. Flights often terminated on three, sometimes two, engines, and the company was getting only 400 engine hours between overhauls. The International Air Transport Association, which in the late forties and fifties exercised a great deal of clout, had given Avianca exactly one year to improve the maintenance department or the airline would lose IATA's sanction for their coveted international routes.

That told me why I had been hired, but I was unprepared for the resistance I would encounter trying to do the job. In spite of my outspoken ways, I had worked well with Latin Americans. To my surprise, Moniño, who had been so friendly when recruiting me, apparently expected something different than what he got. He became the source of ill-concealed staff resentment that trickled down to the anti-*gringo* personnel. Some Colombians to this day haven't forgiven the United States for the loss of territory in the Panama Canal deal. At the outset I had exactly two things going for me: a passing knowledge of Spanish, although I didn't yet speak it well, and the unqualified support of Avianca's president in Bogotá.

If I hadn't already been warned, my first visit to the engine shop with Moniño would have been a real shock. He introduced me to Sr. Gomez, the man in charge of the shop, who never was called anything other than "the old Maestro" because he had run the shop for fourteen years. In Spanish, which he didn't realize I understood, Moniño told him not to worry about it because I wouldn't be around for long, and it wasn't his idea to bring me there in the first place.

Conditions reminded me of the Boulton-Paul factory in England. The production lines were inefficient, the shops dirty, and bad sanitary conditions prevailed in the tropical heat. General disinterest in doing anything the right way, especially if the suggestion came from me, was exhibited by the unskilled Indian workers, company relatives, and general misfits Avianca had managed to employ.

I had just started looking things over when I met George Gonzales, the executive vice-president of Avianca, who asked for an appraisal of the situation. I hoped that he, at least, would be a friend. It took me an hour to describe a mess that in the U.S. would have prompted the CAA to suspend operations immediately.

Moniño looked uncomfortable while Gonzales listened thoughtfully, then told us that an Avianca DC-4 carrying a full load of passengers had just been forced to return to New York on two feathered engines. The pilot had quit and reported the incident to IATA, which was about to send some representatives to Colombia with a threat to withdraw their support for Avianca's landing rights on international routes.

It was imperative to show IATA that the airline was serious about improvements. We sent as many engines as we could load into a DC-4 to Miami for maintenance at Aircraft Service, and shut down the engine shop for remodeling, much of which started with a bulldozer.

When the five IATA people arrived to look at our engine overhaul facilities, I told them what we were doing but admitted we had nothing to show them yet. I didn't understand why that didn't seem to bother them until the Eastern Airlines man in the group reminded me that he had once recommended me for an overhaul contract at Aircraft Services and that Eastern had liked the job we did for them. Considering the problems of the moment, it was nice to hear. As a matter of fact, Eddie Rickenbacker had written me a personal letter of thanks for the work. The meeting convinced IATA that Avianca should have their probationary year, after all.

Meanwhile, I had been making different shop layouts and realized that the Maestro had no conception of what a good production line should be. When I showed him the final layout, he blew his top and went to Sr. Gonzales to protest.

It was time to clear the air. I asked George to translate what I was about to say to the Maestro, because a major decision was involved. I had been hired as a technical advisor, so either we would do things my way for at least a year, or I'd go home and they could go on flying airplanes with unsafe engines. If I stayed, it would be as the Maestro's friend, and perhaps both of us would learn something.

Gonzales told the Maestro to make the decision, but if I left he would fire him the next time there was an engine failure.

The Maestro extended his hand to me and said, "*Amigos?*"

"*Amigos*," I said, and then it was his turn to speak. George translated.

"Mr. Kennedy," he said, "I did not like you and have talked about you, but now you shame me. When you have something to say, you say it in my presence and not behind my back. You are right, but I have been boss of that shop for a long time and I didn't want a younger man replacing me. Now, let's try to put out a good engine together!"

When I got back to the office, he had all the layouts for the new shop pinned to the wall and was ordering his men to finish the job in three days, even if they had to work all night. The Maestro became my ally, sometimes objecting to certain procedures but usually coming around, all the time teaching me how to speak good Spanish every day.

It was Moniño who planted his feet. We had gotten on well in Miami, but apparently he had not foreseen being put in the difficult position of cooperating with a *gringo* who had a free hand in the shops and with whom he totally disagreed on nearly everything.

It came to a head one day when he ordered me to sign a test sheet on an engine I knew wouldn't run for the 1,000 hours minimum we had agreed to. When I refused, he said he'd sign it himself. I told him he couldn't sign off an engine that could fail at any time and go down in the jungle and kill people, adding, "If you sign that sheet it's proof that you don't need me."

"What do you think, Maestro?" Moniño asked.

The Maestro replied "*Siento mucho, jefe, pero yo accordo con el gringo.*"

Nevertheless, I had to threaten to report it to Gonzales and the director of civil aviation before Moniño conceded. The Maestro gave me a bear hug in front of the whole shop and from then on I had the crew's total loyalty. The engine in question had been assembled with the shims mixed up in the master rods. The bearings already were badly scored and about to fail.

IATA lifted its sanction from Avianca as engine performance began to improve, and the company expressed its appreciation in my paycheck. We were getting 1,000 hours on engines and working toward 1,500 hours. They were now operating twenty-four DC-4s, forty-five C-47s, a PBY-5, six C-46s, and a small fleet of Cessna 190s. We had a good maintenance record on all but the Goons.

I was sure this problem lay in improper use of power in flight, not in the maintenance shop. During a conference in Bogotá, Avianca's chief pilot, an American named Bill Brockston, mentioned that the Goons were flown mainly by inexperienced young pilots. Perhaps a non-pilot should fly with them and discretely watch what they were doing aloft.

Most of the C-47s had a combination cargo and passenger configuration, allowing me the pretense of checking loading and tie-downs on inspection flights. I stood behind the pilots, watching instruments and procedures, and indeed they were holding full power too long and ignoring cylinder head temperatures. Nor were they using the cruise power charts.

Brockston sent them back to classes and told them that bad reports would reduce them to co-pilots. By the following year we had a 98.8 percent performance record on the C-47s and 99.4 percent on the DC-4s. Avianca moved from the bottom of the list to second place under KLM. Four years later, they were on top.

While we were working out the engine problems, occasional forced landings required spectacular rescue efforts. One occurred when some cargo sacks were tossed on top of a fully charged battery on a C-47 and fire broke out. The pilot managed to put her down in a shallow lake with the gear touching bottom, and all aboard walked two miles out of the dense jungle to the nearest village. When we surveyed the wreck from the air it looked impossible to get the plane out, but our Colombian mechanics, who knew the country well, thought otherwise. Since we needed the plane, we decided to let them try.

We flew the rescue crew to the nearest open field. From there it was a three-day walk to the lake with a large contingent of workers and a string of pack animals. At the crash site they put huge rubber lifting bags under the partially submerged wings, which were attached to the hull by a total of 927 bolts. The workers soon learned to go underwater and remove three bolts at a time before coming up for air.

The detached wings were floated to the beach and loaded onto native-built dugouts to carry them to a stream running out of the lake. From there it was a long float down to the Magdelena River, where large rafts floated them another 200 miles to Barranquilla.

Next the crew lashed dugouts under the center section and tail of the fuselage and floated it to the beach, where the engines were removed using tripods the natives had built of hardwoods from the forest. Those parts were then floated back to Barranquilla by the same long route. The operation took three and a half months to complete.

From then on, if there was any hope of success we always tried to save a plane, even if it required seemingly impossible procedures. On another occasion a C-47 flew an oil survey crew and their heavy equipment into a small jungle airport completely isolated from outside transportation. The pilot took the plane in 1,500 pounds overweight and ground looped into a thicket of heavy bamboo, ripping off the left wing in two places.

Bill Brockston asked if there was any way we could fasten a new wing to the belly of another Goon and fly it into the field. Dale Smythe and I studied the aircraft's construction and found some strong focal points to which we could attach a fixture to hold the spare wing. We had to disconnect the inboard flaps to do this, which meant the C-47 would have to go in to a short field with only half the required flap area.

They sent us an Avianca pilot who liked to do stunts in a Gooney Bird. He may have been crazy, but he was careful. For three days he practiced landings on a strip we painted off at 3000 feet until he was satisfied he could do it. Then we went up to Bogotá to try it at higher altitude. That felt right, too, so we attached the extra wing to the belly, loaded five mechanics aboard, and off we flew. I was co-pilot. After two short passes over the field to verify wind conditions and field surface, the pilot touched down within 100 feet of the beginning of the runway. This Goon had come in on *three* wings and a prayer!

Once I got the overhaul shops well organized, I had an idea to help the C-47 fleet carry more cargo. There was such a backlog of freight that they were charging extra for priority movement, and without knowing that Avianca was about to bid on a contract to fly equipment and personnel into an emerald mine in the high Andes, I suggested a solution to George Gonzales.

The proposal was to install an R-2000-5 engine and a cut-off DC-4 propeller on the Goon to pull the center of gravity forward. It would permit more cargo aft and increase the take-off weight to at least 30,000 pounds at low altitude airports. At higher altitudes I was sure we could carry nearly 29,000 pounds and still have safe go-around on one engine.

*Three wings and a prayer. Gooney Bird carries a new wing (strapped to belly) to Avianca DC-3 that lost a wing in a ground loop during jungle crash landing. Colombia, early 1950s.*

*Avianca mechanic Eduardo Ramirez with the wrinkled fuselage of the DC-3 floated down the Magdalena River from jungle crash site 200 miles away. Early 1950s.*

George assigned me a permanent test pilot and authorized purchases for anything needed for the conversion. I wondered if this show of confidence precipitated Moniño's abrupt departure shortly thereafter. His replacement was an old-timer from the Medellín base. Antonio Vargas Bustas and I hit it off from the start. No more having to explain why I did things the way I did them.

On test, the first R-2000 had a scoop effect problem, which I corrected by designing a new scoop inspired by the wartime experience on the Boeing B-29. We also ordered DC-4 flying trim tab kits from Douglas to improve control. With a sea level load the Goon got off the ground so well that we kept testing, and even on one engine she easily made the go-around. It appeared the bird would be safe for the mine operation.

As far as I know, putting a R-2000 on a Gooney Bird may have been an airline first. The conversion was eventually approved in the U.S. and I understand some of those planes flew for a long time.

I had been at Avianca for five years and the airline was running smoothly, had gained prestige in the industry, and its well-trained personnel took pride in their work. Tony Bustas had to leave and was replaced by Stan Whiting, an American who was just as pleasant to work with. Consequently, an offer from Robert Anson, manager of the Servicios Aerotechnicos Latino Americanos S.A. maintenance base in Costa Rica, to help straighten out their engine shop was not at first particularly appealing. Polly was stable and happy. We were living well and enjoying Barranquilla, and I liked my job.

The well-known highway contractor Grant Foster had just acquired a major interest in SALA. Subsequently he won the contract to build the difficult stretch of Pan American highway between Costa Rica and Panama. His interest in SALA was strictly pragmatic—he needed an aircraft maintenance organization to support his extensive activities in Central America. He also wanted the IRAN (inspection and repair as necessary) contract from the U.S. Panama Air Command for their C-47s and Bell helicopters. When SALA upped the ante to include a percentage of company profits, I asked for a month to think it over.

Much as we liked living in Colombia, I had begun to question my future with Avianca after a new supervisor came into the maintenance division to replace Stan Whiting. He was the biggest *gringo-*

hater yet. Worse, he was a pilot who knew nothing about maintenance. Before long he was upsetting shop procedures with the announcement that he, not "that Yankee *gringo*," was now running maintenance. With my mentor, George Gonzales, so heavily involved with company affairs in Bogotá and Europe, I had no court of appeal in Barranquilla.

Our total flight hours began to drop off. One night the crew chief came to my house carrying an oil screen from a DC-4, so full of fine brass chips and steel slivers we could separate them with a magnet. I told the chief to change the engine and oil radiator and give the oil tank a thorough cleaning. For some reason, the new man happened to be at the base and heard I had ordered the engine change. There was no way they could change and test the engine in time for the 8:00 run to Miami the next morning. But he had booked himself aboard the flight, and by God that plane was going to go!

My crew reported that he ordered them to "just flush it out and have the plane at the ramp at 8:00. I'll show that *gringo* he can't remove engines just to keep his shop busy while he runs this base!"

I got to work shortly after the plane had taken off, so I rushed to the tower and called him on the radio. He told Pat Passage, the American pilot, to tell me he was busy and we could discuss things when he got back.

"Okay," I said. "But tell him that number three engine is not airworthy and I doubt you'll make it to Jamaica." There was a long silence. Pat's voice was noticeably tense when he came back on the air. He said he had been told I had made the engine change decision while I was drinking and it was necessary to countermand my order.

"I told that bastard I knew you wouldn't do that, so tell me slowly why the engine is bad." He heard me out, then announced that he would climb to altitude, use up some of the fuel load, and return to base. I went back to the office to prepare for the maintenance supervisor's ire at being thwarted in whatever he was planning to do in Miami. I knew he was not scheduled to go there on business.

But it wasn't yet over in the air. An hour later, Pat called me back to the tower. "We're at 15,000 feet. The number three engine is frozen and we can't feather the prop. It's free-wheeling. The nose case has a big split in it and we're afraid everything will fly off and hit either the ship or another engine."

He had tried to dump fuel, but the dumping mechanism was inoperable because parts were missing. I took no satisfaction in remembering that the maintenance supervisor himself had canceled the parts order.

I asked the office to muster emergency equipment to the runway and get fire trucks and ambulances from the city, then told Pat to watch the nose case and do a quick pull-up if it looked like the prop was coming off.

It was a long day for everyone. By 5:00 they were down to landing weight, came in low with full flaps and the gear down, barely missed a five-foot fence, and touched down at the edge of the runway. The passengers quietly filed off, shaken but uninjured. My nemesis passed us without a glance and headed for his office.

I was about ready to go home when he called me in and asked how I knew the engine was that bad.

"Have you ever seen the inside of an engine?" I asked.

"Well, no."

"Look, I knew from experience that the steel slivers they found came from the bearings on the reduction gear in the nose. That's what failed and disconnected the prop shaft and broke the case. You were damned lucky it didn't cut the airplane in half!"

The company had the recording of the cockpit conversation and summoned the supervisor to Bogotá the next day. When he returned he called me in again.

"I got my ass reamed because of you, Kennedy. I still don't like *gringos* and someday I'll get even with you."

"You won't have to," I replied. "I just quit."

I went home and wrote to SALA that I'd be in Costa Rica as soon as we could pack up and catch a flight to San José.

CHAPTER 15

# Pro Tem

POLLY AND I left Barranquilla with heavy hearts. It was not my style to make an abrupt departure without notice, especially while George Gonzales was out of the country. His support when I first went to Avianca had been invaluable, and I was indebted to him for smoothing my path as technical advisor to the company. George was just as unhappy about it, indicating his displeasure some time later in a chilly note refusing my request for a letter of recommendation for a job in the States. He was angry also at SALA for what he perceived as stealing me from Avianca. It was not a good way to terminate a valued association, but at the time I saw no alternative to getting out of an untenable situation.

Our spirits were lifted by the consideration shown by SALA, which had obtained for us a beautiful penthouse apartment in San José. It had a magnificent view, and the only thing we could find to complain about were the earthquakes that periodically jarred the city, making it necessary to hook some of the furniture to the wall.

The situation in the SALA engine overhaul shop was about the same as in other places I'd been sent to reorganize. As I set about making changes, it was good to be working with Latin Americans who were not paranoid about their jobs.

Costa Ricans traditionally like Americans. I already knew and had

*At SALA, San José, Costa Rica, 1955 (left to right): Captain Al Juul, TACA pilot; Art Kennedy, technical consultant; Robert Anson, manager.*

worked with Luís Fernández, SALA's overhaul chief, and, during my twenty months with the company, we became good friends while I trained him to take over and eventually manage the department. Grant Foster got his I.R.A.N. contract with the Panama Air Command, challenging our crew to beef up the operation even more. I had a free hand and Bob Anson, the manager, did his best to cooperate even when he wondered what I was up to.

Bob and I first met when he was ferrying Avianca aircraft to the SALA base for interior conversions and major overhauls on the DC-3s. An excellent pilot, Bob did SALA's test flying, so after I joined the operation I went along as co-pilot to save the company from having to hire one. Because the USAF insisted on a two-hour test for each C-47, we got in a lot of flying with Bob always making me do a couple of touch-and-go's for practice. We also had two Bell helicopters to take care of. The Air Force sent a pilot up from Panama and I got some co-pilot time on those, as well.

Not only was it interesting work, but socially we were making friends who kept us well entertained with Costa Rica's many pleasant diversions. But I was worried about Polly, whose mental problems began to recur. At first, everything we did and saw seemed to thrill her, but as time passed she settled into passive disinterest. The spells came and went. Strangely enough, she was quite normal when we played a lot of tennis. The two of us won the international mixed doubles in a local tournament; then she reached the singles finals until a twisted ankle during the second set took her out of competition. As she became more and more withdrawn, it became apparent I would have to take her back to the States for treatment.

We stayed as long as we could. I was committed to help Grant Foster with his bid on construction of the badly needed El Coco International Airport in Alajuela about twenty-five kilometers from San José. The old airport on the edge of town was an inadequate 4000 feet long, with a 100-foot drop from one end to the other, and no room for extension. El Coco would have a 12,000-foot runway with 2000-foot overruns and unobstructed approaches.

In addition, I was helping to reorganize and modernize the shops SALA would have at El Coco with their expanded maintenance organization. To implement this, I suggested to Luiz that he and his crew make a miniature three-dimensional layout for the shops. They weren't sure why, but obediently turned out the best balsa wood models I had ever seen. Everything was there—work benches, test equipment, tiny quarter-inch scale gauges, even little cleaning buckets and mops.

I let them do it alone, then pointed out where they had forgotten clearance for parts racks moving down aisles and for men bent over at work. Nor had they allowed room for materials and an inspection bench alongside the work layout benches. The project convinced them of the value of the three-dimensional planning system.

Foster won the contract for the airport runways, roads, and parking areas. We were well into planning when Polly's condition grew critical. With great regret, I resigned and took her home. It had been a fulfilling assignment and I was glad to have assisted SALA in becoming the only U.S. CAA-certified commercial foreign repair station in all of Latin America at the time, employing 600 men.

It was February 1956. To my relief, Polly seemed glad to be back in the States. We vacationed in Miami briefly, then she asked if we could visit New York again before we drove back to Burbank. In the bar at the Lexington we ran into an old Curtiss-Wright friend, who slapped me on the back and said, "Where the hell have you been? The company has been looking all over for you!"

Their Caldwell-Wright division was planning to build a large overhaul shop in Southern California to accommodate a big Flying Tiger contract. They wanted me to go out there as works manager.

With the apparent improvement in Polly's condition and her desire to be back in the Los Angeles area, at the time it seemed a good idea to take the job, but I should have known better. The president of the division had asked me to call him, but expected us to cool our heels for five days until he could fit me into his appointment schedule. Only after I told him I was taking my wife back to California the next day whether I had a job or not did he find time to see me. When he did, we had a stormy interview during which he told me he didn't like my independent attitude. I was surprised he still wanted me on the job.

It was not an auspicious beginning, but the division president turned out to be the least of the problems. Even before I reported to the Burbank airport area to start work, the project had been plagued with bad company politics, ineptness, union problems, falsified inspection reports, and deliberate sabotage. I knew my employers were well informed about my blunt but—knock wood—so far successful methods. They knew that in every shop I ever ran, the failure rate hovered around only 2 percent. Their East Coast operation was hobbling along at 14 percent, which is why they wanted me to help build the new West Coast facility. But, in effect, support at the executive level, where I had been promised "a free hand," was seriously eroded by their staffing the project with unsuitable personnel.

It was obvious I was in the wrong place at the wrong time, yet my chronic stubborn pride kept me from taking the prudent course and resigning early in the game. I stuck with it for a year and a half, until we got the facility built and running. It required working long hours under a lot of strain, and one night I passed out on the production floor. At St. Joseph's Hospital in Burbank they determined that it was not a heart attack, but extreme fatigue. I was released with orders to take it easy and went back to work, where personnel problems continued to mount.

It's only fair to acknowledge that the company tangibly expressed its appreciation for my work with a sizable, supposedly confidential Christmas incentive award for more than fulfilling their original expectations. But its unauthorized revelation to other personnel led to an attempted engine sabotage that was supposed to get me fired. What it got was my resignation. Shortly after that the division president died of a heart attack, then production got so bad that the Flying Tigers finally took their business to TWA in Kansas City. The whole venture had been a brutal and costly fiasco.

I would need another job, but where? For three weeks I rested while Polly and I assessed our future. She seemed to have recovered from her setbacks—still undiagnosed—even as I was experiencing professional problems, so I was glad to hear her suggest that we go back to South America. "We're always happy there," she said, and I had to agree.

No sooner had I made the decision than E.B. Edmonds, a Miami friend who worked for Varig Airlines, telephoned to ask if I'd like to go to Brazil for a month to investigate some engine and schedule problems at Varig. It would pay well and possibly lead to a longer assignment. Well acquainted with Brazilian laundry facilities, Polly packed up more than the month's supply of wash-and-wear clothing and drove me to LAX.

When I got to New York, E.B. and Don Cardiff, a former Varney pilot now in charge of Varig's New York operations, met me with a contract signed by Reuben Berta, president of Varig. It guaranteed a free hand to investigate the airline operation and prepare a written report within the week. During the two-hour layover Don filled me in on some of the problems, including an appalling 80 percent delay on international flights.

Recalling the length of that flight to Pôrto Alegre in a Constellation L1049 makes one appreciate today's jet travel. It took twenty-six hours to fly from New York with stops at Trinidad, Belém, Rio, and finally our destination.

My old friend Jerry Mass from Cruzeiro do Sul days was in charge of Varig's engine shop. The day I reported for work he accompanied me to the airport, on the way relating Varig's troubles, which seemed so extensive that I felt sorry for him before we even got to the plant. There he introduced me to the staff, a friendly bunch for the most part except for some ill-concealed hostility in the engineering department. However I soon found a real friend in Hans Volke, the vice president in charge of purchasing, who seemed to have a lot of clout in every department.

It didn't take more than a week to figure out what needed to be done. It was serious enough that I told Berta he shouldn't wait for the written report. He called a staff meeting and listened to my suggestions for some immediate major changes if they really wanted to get their overhaul into reliable production.

The three requirements were that there must be one supervisor whose word is absolutely final, the shops needed to be re-layed out, and the inspection department needed to be reorganized, removed from the engineering department, and put under the chief of maintenance.

The latter suggestion, for which I had become infamous in the industry, never went over well with engineers. Nevertheless it always worked. Berta didn't need convincing. He knew the airline business, having been with Varig since it was founded in 1927 by the Condor Syndikat as a local service carrier with the top-heavy name Empresa de Viação Aérea Rio Grandense. Starting as a nineteen-year-old ticket seller and bookkeeper, Berta had climbed through the ranks to reach the presidency of the airline.

Having heard the preliminary report, Berta directed me to spend the remainder of the month helping to initiate needed changes in the shops. I also made it a point to be on the ramp and in the hangars three or four hours a day. Some of the engineering types seemed cool, but I was used to that, and Hans Volke was a good ally. Many of the changes could not be effected under present personnel, but I was learning to keep my mouth shut until the right time. It would be better to insert those findings in the written report.

Berta was adamant about putting his airline into the big league. No expenditure was too much, no change too radical. I noted a serious flaw in service on the long flights, where four attendants were inadequate to serve passengers properly on the Constellation L-1049. I suggested that Varig add three girls to their staff of four attendants, plus a hostess. This would speed up service, but it also was an opportunity to try something I'd been thinking about for a long time—rolling trays for drinks and food.

Berta later told me Varig was the first to use rolling carts, but I've never been able to verify that. Others would have thought of it sooner or later, but perhaps we did help pioneer better food service. I do know that when we later introduced food and drink self-service from the carts, thank you letters poured into Varig, which shortly acquired a reputation for fantastic service aloft. Before long they carried most of the traffic between Rio and New York.

When I completed the investigation and submitted the written report, Berta was in Europe. The report was pretty rough and I was just as glad not to be around when he read it, so I flew back to New York and hid out at the Roosevelt Hotel instead of the usual aviation haunts at the Lexington. Somehow, Don Cardiff tracked me down and at four o'clock in the morning telephoned to say that Mr. Berta wanted me on the next afternoon's flight back to Pôrto Alegre.

It was impossible, I told him. For one thing I needed to get home to Polly. For another, I was reluctant to face Berta in light of the critical report.

"He read me your report," Don said. "He says to tell you he concurs with everything you said, even to firing his top maintenance people and all their relatives at the main base." To paraphrase an old popular song, there was an awful lot of nepotism in Brazil.

Polly, apparently her old self again and raring to go, already had been contacted about coming down to join me, had agreed, and was packed. Berta offered a four-month contract with the possibility of a permanent position if he could get permission from the Brazilian government.

I booked on the next return flight and was surprised when Berta himself met me in Pôrto Alegre. He told me to finish with the engine and accessory shops and help reorganize the maintenance department. We were to continue with the innovations on service aloft, and, while all this was going on, I was to be thinking about staying permanently. We decided to defer that decision for a while because, among other reasons, the Brazilian *cruzeiro* was dropping in value.

After Polly arrived the company installed us in a suite at the Hotel Umbu. She was pleased to be back in Brazil and started playing tennis again. We made new friends, traveled throughout the region, and feasted royally on good pampas-fed beef accompanied by marvelous wines from the nearby Caixis vineyards. Life had become an adventure again, and we thought we could be happy in this part of Brazil forever.

In two months the maintenance department was completely revamped. By the third month we had only one short delay getting a plane to the depot and only one engine rejection in the test cell. At the end of five months things were going well, although Varig still had a long haul to peak efficiency. I had many ideas for further improvement, but the time had come to talk about staying or leaving. Just as Berta offered a five-year contract, the Brazilian *cruzeiro* plunged again and he was unable to get government approval to pay me in dollars. He had to be careful about that, because the airline's access to dollars from U.S. ticket sales kept the Brazilian government constantly peering over Berta's shoulder. The best he could do, by cheating a little, was 25 percent of the salary deposited in dollars in New York and the rest paid in *cruzeiros* at the highest rate for an alien technician.

Polly and I considered carefully, but we couldn't have lived on the offered salary in the manner to which we had become accustomed, so I thanked Berta but said I had to decline. He was one of the world's true gentlemen and I hated to turn him down, feeling even worse about it when he sent Polly and me on a luxurious all-expenses-paid, ten-day vacation in Montevideo, Uruguay. We returned to Pôrto Alegre to pick up our things and the morning after Berta hosted a beautiful farewell party for us, flew to New York and home to California.

Neither of us knew that it was the last time Polly would ever see her beloved South America. Nor had we the slightest inkling that our next adventure together lay in the velvet-clad paw of Africa's Lion of Judah.

CHAPTER 16

# Ethiopia

ON OCTOBER 3, 1958, Polly and I arrived in California. On October 5, TWA's office in Kansas City telephoned to say they'd heard I was back from Brazil and how would I like to go to Addis Ababa for three years with Ethiopian Airlines?

I was forty-five years old, and for nearly thirty years of my life I had been learning and teaching the fine skill of nurturing aircraft engines. Jobs had more or less come looking for me, seemingly at just the right time. Now we were presented with another extraordinary opportunity. Anxious about Polly, however, I talked with her at some length about the implications of unaccustomed living conditions in Africa. She seemed to have made a complete recovery during our stay in Brazil, and urged me to take the job.

TWA was familiar with my work, but I understood why the interview and "management test" required of prospective employees was necessary. Ethiopia's vastly different cultural climate could be a challenge to any American sent to work with Haile Selassie's thirteen-year-old airline. It was a challenge, however, to be welcomed by anyone who was devoted to work in commercial aviation, for reasons best stated by John Gunther in *Inside Africa*:

"One of the most remarkable airlines in the world. More than any force except the emperor knits the country together. Ethiopian Airlines has flown in Ethiopia under day-in, day-out circumstances that would make any official of the Civil Aeronautics Board faint, sob, or cut his throat, without a single fatal accident."

When we met together in Kansas City, a cluster of TWA executives explained to me that they were looking for a versatile technician to organize, teach, and maintain quality control on accessories (brakes, landing gear, propellers, etc.), one also experienced in engine overhaul. The airline's future plans also called for consultation on layout for a new airport four years hence, including a study for requirements of the Boeing 720s expected to join the Ethiopian Airlines fleet.

The management test, basically an intensely probing interview, lasted four hours, after which they sent me out for a three-hour lunch while they evaluated the results and made a decision.

When I returned to the conference room three solemn men silently waited for me to be seated. I thought I had failed to meet their management criteria.

"Mr. Kennedy, we were supposed to ask you more questions about the work you would be involved in, but after checking your answers we have decided to forego that. We want you on our staff!" With that, they broke out in broad smiles and explained that my score was so high they thought I'd had access to the test until they checked and learned I arrived in Kansas City only the night before.

They offered the highest salary for a TWA overseas mission. We were to leave in two weeks, so while Polly packed I reluctantly sold our beloved Oldsmobile 88 Holiday, which never would have survived Ethiopian roads, and on the advice of a TWA man just back from Addis ordered a new Borgward Isabella to be shipped from Frankfurt to Addis Ababa.

Arriving in Addis, we took temporary quarters at the Hotel Ghion and I reported to "Simmy" Simpson, the airline's director of maintenance under whom I would be working. He immediately took me on a tour of the shops; when I wondered aloud how airplanes could fly out of shops so badly equipped, Simmy said, "That's why you're here, Kennedy."

In 1958 Ethiopian Airlines was flying DC-6s, DC-3s, Convair 440s, and Hiller Bell helicopters on routes that, by 1960, took EAL into Egypt, the Arabian Peninsula, and Europe. Their biggest delays were coming from malfunctioning accessories. I asked how much authority I would have to correct the problems. Simmy laughed.

"New people usually first ask about food, houses, and where they can buy things. You sound like you're ready to start!" I suggested that TWA's version of the Welcome Wagon should get in touch with my wife, who would handle our living arrangements, and I would start in the accessory shop in the morning. He shook my hand. "I think you and I are going to get along fine!"

The shops were worse than I realized, dirty and badly laid out. Simmy agreed to shut them down for a week or so and the next day the whole crew, including myself, were washing down the floors and sweeping a mess of cobwebs off walls and ceilings.

Evidently I got off to a good start with the Ethiopians because I wore khakis and worked alongside them. Not until one of them mentioned that I was the only *franji* who did that did I look around and see that other managers came to work in coats and ties. Simmy only smiled when I asked if I was doing the wrong thing and dismissed me with, "Stop worrying about what the others think!"

We got the shops clean and painted the walls. I made a new layout and recalibrated the test benches; gradually the place began to look like a production shop.

Simmy came to inspect and made a nice little speech to the workers about how good it looked and that he hoped they would keep it that way. One of the Ethiopians said, "Mr. Simpson, I do not think you have to worry. Mr. Kennedy told us if we did not keep it clean he would put one of us on cleaning detail each week and that person would not be able to get any training or work on any units."

Ethiopians are very proud. The threat of being put on cleaning detail had made a big impression, because it also meant they couldn't eat with their comrades. This kind of punishment was common for the slightest disgrace, as I learned later on when one of my workers had to borrow a little money from me. As soon as he could, he walked thirty kilometers to my home to repay it. Then, he told us, he could eat with his family once more.

At Simmy's request, the two of us made a discrete survey of EAL's physical operation and turned up a number of bad situations that he immediately ordered corrected. Few outside the industry realize how much care must be taken in shops that naturally seem to create dirt and a mess. For instance, the welding shop needed to be sealed off from an area where they were doping ailerons and elevators, in order to alleviate a dangerous fire hazard. Other shops were cleaned and painted and the sandblast area was moved out of the engine shop. Disassembly and cleaning operations were separated from the production line, and a set of double doors installed to dustproof the instrument shop. Ventilation fans were installed in the dope shop and wash and paint stripping racks moved to the other side of the main hangar with covered drains. Ground equipment was washed and repainted, and leaking jacks repaired.

We began to keep better records for inspection, assembly, and testing procedures, and I taught each mechanic how to rework old parts instead of automatically ordering new stock. At the end of six months the delays for which the accessories shops had been responsible were reduced to almost zero.

The next gauntlet to be run was my first annual budget encounter with Victor H. Harrell, Jr., the airline's general manager. Everyone cautioned me to insert something extra into the budget because Harrell was a tough bastard who would make you take something out no matter what, just for the hell of it.

I worked on mine for three weeks. Simmy thought it was a good budget but was sure Harrell would cut it to pieces. He sat in quiet amusement while I listened first to congratulations on my accomplishments and then a dissertation on the airline needing to tighten its belt in the coming year. Having set the stage, Harrell picked up my budget and said, "Before we start, do you want to see if you can cut out anything?"

"Hell, no," I said. "I spent a lot of time on this and I know from past experience that I have been economical and these things are what I need."

He checked the budget item by item, making a note by each one, and handed it back to me with a smile.

"You know this is ridiculous, Art. You can do better. Take this and come back with a better budget."

"No," I said. "That's what I need and I'm not going over it again because it will come out the same."

Harrell was not pleased. "A tough guy, eh?"

"No, just practical."

"Well, I won't accept it this way, so what do you say to that?"

"That's easy. It's your airline, and if you like delays and enroute failures you can cut the budget as you wish. But I won't accept any responsibility if you do it."

I was just warming up.

"And don't give me that nonsense about the airline being hard up. You forget I'm not like the rest of the TWA people. I've had experience in many airlines and I know when it's running well or not. The DC-6 on this run breaks even at 39 percent payload and for over a year yours has averaged 88 percent a month. The DC-3s break even at 34 percent and you've been carrying full loads plus double headers to Yemen and the interior. The helicopters break more than even at less than $400 an hour, and you've been charging the government $950 on the water survey project alone. You've got a 140-hour-a-month guarantee whether you fly or not. So stop the bullshit."

Harrell looked at Simmy. "Well, you warned me he was different, but you didn't tell me he was so goddamn cocky."

"Look, it's your airline. Sign my budget or release me. You need me and I don't need you, period."

"Calm down, Art," he laughed. "I was just trying you out, and I must say I like your attitude. Here!" He signed the budget, gave me a copy, and said, "Get out of here and go back to work while I scare the hell out of the others!"

During the time I was learning, again, to survive the company politics of American management, Polly and I were getting to know the immensely likable Ethiopian people. We began a unique association with them when some of my workers asked if I would teach them how to draw. Apparently they were impressed by the drawings of accessories I had made when assembling maintenance manuals. I possess a modest talent but no formal art training, and I certainly was no art teacher. They were so eager, though, that I agreed to try if they would come to my house twice a week.

I bought enough drawing paper and charcoal for everybody and on the first appointed Tuesday night set up the easel. Promptly at eight o'clock the doorbell rang and fifteen young Ethiopians, including three girls I had never seen before, filed in. We possessed only five chairs, but they happily sat on the floor as we started with charcoal free-hand drawings. They worked diligently, and at ten o'clock Polly and I had to sweep them out the door with the promise of another class the following Thursday.

During the fourth week of lessons, a well-dressed Ethiopian gentleman appeared and asked to watch. He sat silently until the end of class, then stood and spoke in flawless Oxford English.

"Mr. Kennedy and students, I must say that I am more than impressed with what I have seen. Daj Mekian, here," pointing to a pretty but extremely shy girl, "has been showing us at the palace her improvements and we were very interested."

We had no idea either of them was from the palace!

"I personally have talked with every student here, and I am pleased that only eight of them are from the airline and that you have accepted people from other walks of life."

We hadn't known that, either!

"We also are aware that you pay for the materials out of your own pocket. I wish to advise you that His Majesty has authorized me to tell you to buy your equipment from the paint shop in the square and everything for you and the classes will be paid for by the palace."

The students, who had been sitting quietly, all smiles, broke into applause.

"His Majesty wants me to convey to you his personal thanks for accepting his people into your home and giving them what they cannot get in our school system. He appreciates your interest in his people, because you are the first *franji* that has come to Addis and done this."

He sat down. Polly and I were so overcome we were speechless, and the truth finally dawned. Our guest was one of the princes! Ethiopia's benevolent despot had his eye on us.

The palace's interest remained at first low-keyed, however, and there was little evidence of it as I pursued my part in the airline business at hand under the three-year contract. Other TWA people came and went from Addis Ababa constantly, some to help, others to take advantage of a free trip to Africa. One young power plant engineer from the States, whom I looked upon as another know-it-all without any practical experience, got mixed up in my Q.E.C. department. I had it well organized with a good Ethiopian chief, but this guy always seemed to be looking for something to find fault with. Probably I've always been too sensitive about not having a college degree, but by now I had come to the conclusion that Engineer-Technician Conflict 101 must be a required course in the aeronautical engineering curriculum.

I had to go to Europe to track down spares, and instructed the chief of the Q.E.C. shop to build up two R-1830 engines for a bird soon due out of major overhaul. The new engineer told me not to worry, he'd be glad to keep an eye on the department while I was gone, which was exactly my biggest worry. I asked him not to make any changes until I got back.

The R-1830s were finished and installed on the bird on schedule. Someone mentioned that the engineer had made one small change, but I wasn't alert enough to ask what it was.

Two weeks went by before we got the MAYDAY from this bird. The pilot reported both engines had quit. Fortunately, he was on the plains and could go in without trouble.

Simmy immediately summoned us and asked why two engines would go out at once. Nobody had an answer, but while he was showing us a map something kept going through my mind, and suddenly I went cold. I called in the kid power plant engineer.

"When I left," I told him, "I gave instructions to you not to change anything, right?"

"Yes, but it wasn't a change. If I hadn't spotted it they would have left it out."

"Yeah? And what was that?"

"They forgot to install the ice screens on top of the carburetor."

"They forgot like hell!" I yelled. "What did the Q.E.C. chief say to you?"

"He just said they never use the ice screens, but Art you know as well as I do you don't need cold weather to get ice. So I told them to put them on."

I snatched the map out of Jimmy's hand and pointed to the cross-hatching in the area where the plane went down. Simmy suddenly knew what I was getting at. Cross-hatching on a chart indicated a heavy locust area.

He was about to throw the kid out of the office when the tower called to say the plane was in one piece and the crew uninjured.

Simmy ordered two Cessnas to ferry four mechanics and their tools out to the plain to remove the cowling and scoops from the downed aircraft. To the kid Simmy said, innocently enough, "And *you* are going with them. When the cowling and scoop are off you are going to get in and clean the locusts off the top of those screens, and then you will remove those damned ice screens and get your ass back here as soon as possible."

For some reason the kid was afraid of being attacked by elephants, but the closest herd already had been reported fifty miles away and moving out of the area. His alternatives were to go out there and do what he was told or get on the next plane to Kansas City.

Ice screens on aircraft piston engines prevent large pieces of ice from hitting the blower and damaging the blades. However, in locust country, the four-inch critters pile up on the screen and block the air flow to the engine, causing total failure. With no ice screens to stop them the locusts go through the venturis into the blower and burn up in the combustion. The engine simply digests them. That's why we left the ice screens off.

In this case the locusts were piled six inches deep on top of the screens. The poor engineer got so sick to his stomach trying to dig them out that he couldn't finish the job. He came back and resigned, saying he wouldn't work where non-engineers were allowed to overrule him.

Simmy called him in for a heart-to-heart talk. "Look," he said, "you've had no practical experience. Art may not be an aeronautical engineer, but he's been in this racket over thirty years. He's worked in a lot of strange places and knows about adapting to conditions. Now why don't you tear up the resignation? Maybe we can make a real engineer out of you and when you go back to the States you will be of more value to the industry."

He was smart enough to take the advice and became a real asset to the company. Simmy saved a good man for the aviation industry, and I learned some forbearance, remembering another cocky kid who had to face some hard growing-up lessons.

Well into the second year of our contract, Simmy called a meeting and informed us that in two days His Imperial Majesty, Emperor Haile Selassie I, was coming to see our shops and learn what we were doing to train his people. It was imperative that we all should make a good impression.

The man in charge of the engine shop fancied himself an undiscovered comic talent. As usual, he was the first to comment.

"Hey, this guy doesn't know anything about the technical and we can easily pull the wool over his eyes. I'll prove it. I'll show him the shop and make up some screwball explanations and he'll never know the difference."

A German manager who had been in Ethiopia for several years warned, "You do what you like, but Haile Selassie is no fool and I'm going to give it to him straight."

The clown laughed and said, "Okay, fellows, do as you wish, but I'm going to have some fun."

Early in the morning of the appointed day, Haile Selassie strode in, trailed by an assortment of little princes in gray flannel Eton suits and fifteen attendants dressed to kill. The entourage was escorted by an honor guard, each of the resplendently uniformed officers leading a lion on a chain.

The staff followed his Royal Highness through the shops, myself among them taking photographs as the supervisors explained what went on there. But few of them told what his people were taught to do. When we got to the comedian's shop, the performance was acutely embarrassing. His Majesty rolled his eyes in disapproval as our man made an ass of himself trying to scam the airline's owner, who indeed was no fool.

By the time he got to our accessories shops, the emperor was in ill humor. I said, "Your Majesty, my approach will be a little different, as I do not intend to show you the shops, but rather let each worker explain in your language what he does."

His Majesty's mood improved. He soon put my men at ease and one boy took him to his equipment and demonstrated how he tested a fuel pump. After that the emperor went from man to man, chatting in Amheric with each, and now and then he would glance sideways at me. At the end, he thanked me for a pleasant demonstration and then asked where I was from, how long I had been in aviation and TWA, and was I happy here. He then shook my hand and wished me much happiness and a long life.

As several noses were out of joint because I was the only one His Majesty personally addressed, I brushed it off as only a polite termination to his visit, which I honestly thought was the case. Two days later, however, the emperor walked in to my shop, alone except for a

*Emperor Haile Selassie and Ethiopian Airlines personnel during inspection of parts shop, Addis Ababa, 1960.*

magnificent male lion on a lead. Palace lions were a domesticated breed and as docile as house cats. Nevertheless, they were imposing beasts and made even a man of Haile Selassie's diminutive stature seem to stand twelve feet tall.

He greeted me by name and held out his hand to present me with a beautiful gold ring carved with a figure of the Lion of Judah. Without further conversation he then asked to go to the engine shop so he could talk with the workers again. The comedian manager approached, but was waved off as the emperor spoke intently with the Ethiopians.

When that breathtaking event was over, Simmy told me that His Majesty was happy as a lark. "He also asked me to be sure that *you* are happy and will stay with Ethiopian Airlines." I said I thought that had a slightly ominous sound to it. Simmy did little to dispel the impression.

"So far he had never interfered with what we do, but this was a request we must consider to be an order. He also told us to send the engine shop man back to the U.S.A. with a message: 'Quit trying to fool people because they will soon know you are the biggest fool.' "

For all his royal trappings, Haile Selassie cared deeply about his country's future. He was a conservationist, and in that role was indirectly responsible for our meat supply. No trophy hunters were permitted in Ethiopia, but an Armenian named Marker, who worked for me, was at the time the one white man granted a hunting license. Occasionally a rogue elephant, lion, or cheetah would attack a village and the government would send for Marker to dispatch it. In payment he was allowed to hunt for kudos, wart hogs, dick-dick, and antelope,

*Aerial view of Ethiopian Airlines airport facilities, 1960.*

but only for meat. Killing for skins was forbidden. Thanks to Marker we ate more wild game than domesticated cattle, which was very tough, anyway, and seldom on our menu.

A frequent flyer, the emperor had priority on a DC-6 whenever he wanted to travel. It was, after all, his airline. When notice came from the palace, the crew converted the aft section of the aircraft to an elaborate throne room with Persian carpets on the floor and couches straight out of *The Arabian Nights*. The front of the plane was sectioned off with curtains woven of solid gold threads, and furnished with enormous overstuffed chairs. Fit for a king, indeed!

Late in 1961 His Majesty boarded his sumptuous aircraft and departed on a state journey to Rio de Janeiro. The Army took advantage of the emperor's absence to storm the palace, killing some of his family and all the officials there in an attempted coup. The Ethiopian Air Force and Royal Guards fought back, and because both sides had plentiful arms and ammunition it turned into a real war. Before it was over, at least 50,000 people were dead, although the statistic never was admitted in news accounts.

When the shooting first started we were told to get the hell out of the airport and go home. Trying to secure the airfield, Simmy and I were the last to leave as rebel soldiers stormed in to close off the runways with oil barrels and our rolling stock. Royal Guards were machine-gunning them down, but I was too scared to stay around and watch. I ran for the car and took off. At the airport gate four of my workers flagged me down. They knew an old back road to town. Shots buzzed past the car as they piled in. The little Borgward had never been so mistreated, but she took the bumps on that dirt trail like a trouper. I kept my foot on the floorboard, and when we got to the corner near my apartment on Churchill Avenue the Ethiopians dove out. Our night guard had the garage doors open, I shot in like a racing pro, and he slammed the doors shut.

Polly, who often worked at American embassies or consulates when we lived abroad, was on duty in our embassy code room and unable to get home. Before dark a messenger came to assure me that everybody there was safe, but would have to stay the night. The compound was located between a royal house and the Army, and all night long the two factions lobbed shells at each other over the American embassy. Churchill Avenue was a battleground, too, tracers flying past the window in both directions. Only my laundry and I knew how frightening it was.

The next morning one of the Royal Guards, along with a member of the opposition, came to the door and told me to stay away from the windows. All combatants had agreed to set up four 50 calibre machine guns on either side of the building to ensure that no whites were hurt. Killing a white person would bring unwelcome international attention to their little war.

After two days the firing lessened and Polly was escorted home. The Army had placed a howitzer and a rocket launcher in a deep ravine next to us. One afternoon I was looking out the window when an airplane came low up the ravine, firing into the Army installation. He pulled up, still firing, and just missed the roof of our apartment. A bullet came through the window at eye level eight inches from my head and buried itself in our living room wall. So much for curiosity. We spent the next six days either cowering on the floor or sleeping on mattresses in the living room, where a concrete balcony and bookshelves below the windows would, I hoped, stop stray bullets. The one bullet we did take was dug out, mounted in Ethiopian gold, and added to Polly's charm bracelet.

As soon as the firing stopped Polly and I stocked up for expected contingencies and I went back to work. The Royal Guards had killed every one of the rebels who came that first day to close the airport. Shoes and uniform buttons were all that remained of them because hyenas had eaten them as fast as they fell. Most of our Ethiopian workers had lost at least one family member, and two of our top men were missing.

Our first task was to clear the runway, at which point a message came that His Majesty was flying in. Royal Guards and the Air Force had stopped the coup.

As if that were not enough excitement, heavy earthquakes began to shake Addis Ababa every few hours, and didn't stop for several weeks. They were strong enough to damage 80 percent of the buildings in the city, including our own. We moved to an apartment built on top of a granite mound where earthquakes could not move it. The unpleasantness in the Congo added to our discomfort. It was reflected in the behavior of many Ethiopians, who began to look askance at all whites and before long were spitting on them in the street. We were genuinely fond of these intelligent, handsome people, and were saddened to watch the country undergo an upheaval that would change it forever.

Polly and I agreed that it was time to leave. My three-year contract was nearly at an end, so I told Simmy I wouldn't be renewing it. He understood, but asked me to stay long enough to put the finishing touches on shop plans for the new airport. New Boeing 720s were expected within the year.

I was researching facilities for jet engine maintenance and was interested in the project, but nevertheless informed Simmy that we were preparing to leave Ethiopia at a moment's notice as soon as the contract was up.

We sold every non-essential, including the faithful little Borgward, which the Ethiopian buyer said I could use until we left. We had been very quiet about it, but one day the heir apparent to the throne summoned me to Simmy's office. Simmy signaled that I should be very careful about what I said. First the prince asked if I was happy in Addis, to which I quickly replied, "Oh, yes. Why?"

"We are interested in why you are selling all your things, since you have been requested to stay for another five years."

"I know, but according to my contract, at the end of three years I am entitled to bring in a new car and furniture for an extended stay. We're going to take our vacation in Germany and buy new things."

"If that is the case, I would like to buy your furniture and all your carpets," he replied, "and any dishes or kitchen utensils you intend to sell. I will come to your house next week and we can settle on a price, so please do not sell anything else."

I assured him of our cooperation and thought the conversation was finished. But he added, "You have impressed His Majesty very much, Mr. Kennedy. He has no intention of losing you. You may have noticed that the area and grounds where you live have not been molested. That is because you live there. The new guards and gardeners are from the palace are well trained to ensure your safety."

In addition to the other discomforts we were experiencing, it was unnerving to live under Haile Selassie's protective custody. He meant business. A military jeep followed me to the airport every morning, and Polly and I were watched closely wherever we went.

We carried on as normally as we could, Simmy agreeing to sign me

*Author is shown photographing prince and palace entourage in accessories shop, Ethiopian Airlines, 1960.*

out for vacation when we were ready to leave and to provide two first-class tickets to Los Angeles. The prince came to the apartment and paid a good price in dollars for everything we had left and asked for first refusal on our new furnishings when we departed five years hence. We promised he could have them.

His interest in our modest belongings was not as strange as it may seem. Even the royal family was not exempt from Haile Selassie's edict against buying imported goods if the same items were made in Ethiopia, so everybody snapped up the superior consumer goods left behind by departing Europeans and Americans.

Polly and I decided this was a good opportunity to buy a European car to take home. The Mercedes agency in Addis Ababa was about to lose its franchise on the 190 SL sport convertible, palace business having sharply fallen off, and they needed to sell one soon. We could have one for $3,800. All we had to do was pick it up at the factory. Simmy was willing to trade the Frankfurt-Los Angeles portion of our airline tickets for boat tickets for us and the car, sailing from Seville to New York.

Everything finally was in order. On January 3, 1962, we quietly boarded an EAL airliner and slipped out of Addis Ababa, a beautiful city named "beautiful flower." As we buckled into our seats, twelve Ethiopian friends came aboard to say goodbye, each of them holding a farewell flower which they handed to Polly. There were tears in their eyes.

We wept, too, as we flew away. At first invisible when we began our African adventure, the claws of the Lion of Judah had worked their way through the velvet glove, and we knew we could never return as long as Haile Selassie ruled Ethiopia. Yet we took with us a great treasure, the forever haunting memories of three years in a magnificent country among magnificent people.

And, of course, the emperor's gold ring, which I wear to this day.

CHAPTER 17

# Portuguese Landing

SHORTLY BEFORE WE LEFT ADDIS, I played golf with a lieutenant colonel attached to the Military Assistance Advisory Group (MAAG) there and confided that we were going to leave and I would be looking for a job in the U.S. He stopped in mid-drive and asked me not to make a decision before contacting a friend of his at Torrejon Air Base near Madrid. When we got to Spain I called on the gentleman, very casually, and was offered a temporary job with the U.S. Air Force Contract Administration Office at the Oficinas Generais Materia Aeronáutica, the Portuguese Air Force maintenance base near Lisbon.

The Air Force seemed anxious to make a deal, but we were having too good a time touring Europe in our little jewel of a Mercedes to give the job much more thought until the morning we and the SL were to sail from Seville on a Swedish freighter. As we were packing, Polly suddenly announced that she did not want to go back to the United States. She seemed fearful and repeatedly reminded me that my last Stateside job had put me in the hospital. She thought if I took the six-month position with the USAF it would give us an address in Europe while I looked for a job that would make us both happy. Because Polly always made such good sense, I ignored the nagging suggestion that her almost frantic fear might signal the beginning of another relapse and agreed that we should remain in Europe.

We canceled the passage to Miami and drove back to Madrid, where I contacted JUSMAG (Joint U.S. Military Advisory Group) and told them I had reconsidered. The colonel in charge was so pleased that I was afraid he was going to kiss me. They were in deep trouble in Lisbon. I was cleared for Civil Service GS-11 Step 3 and told to report to Colonel Kenneth Juhn at Alverca, near Lisbon, which I did on April 23, 1962.

Since 1958, the United States Air Force had used this prime Portuguese maintenance base to overhaul DC-3s belonging to our European, African, and Asian embassies, and occasionally worked on DC-4s from other bases. The U.S. Department of Defense was supposed to provide two Civil Service GS-11s for production and quality control, but little semblance of either quality or control was in evidence when I reported for work. Aircraft were stacked up on the tarmac awaiting attention. It was so bad that the USAF was on the verge of terminating its IRAN contract with the Portuguese Air Force.

Very soon after signing on, I had to tell Col. Juhn that most of their operations were as useless as tits on a boar, and the first thing we should do was ask for a conference with OGMA's commanding officer, Fernando de Oliveira. Juhn set it up immediately. General Oliveira seemed to be impressed by my knowledge of aircraft production and asked intelligent questions about my experience. The conference started at eight in the morning; by the end of the day the general was ready to reorganize the Portuguese operation, clearly as anxious as the U.S. was to beef up the operation.

The Portuguese Air Force assigned some good men to help us. One was Lt. Francisco Quina, a graduate aeronautical engineer educated in England. Xico's willingness to learn, and his faultless English, were of great assistance and we're still good friends. His Portuguese classmate, Lt. Rui Espandinha, also came to us as an engineer. Today he is a three-star general and the director of OGMA.

The combined efforts of our military and the Portuguese saved the U.S. Air Force IRAN contract. At the end of six months, Department of Defense personnel came to Lisbon with a group of officers from JUSMAG and presented me with a contract for another year and a Civil Service upgrade that amounted to a ten-year promotion. As the chief of JUSMAG boarded the aircraft to leave, he shook my hand and wondered if any other USAF bases in Europe had such a versatile maintenance man who was a "damn good pilot," as well.

The remark made me a little nervous. Apparently the word had gotten out that I was flying co-pilot with Colonel Juhn. Portuguese personnel were supposed to co-pilot on test flights, but one day he needed to get a DC-4 back to the Army in a hurry. The only qualified Portuguese pilot was in Angola, so the colonel simply filled in a Portuguese name on the log and took me along instead—from then until he left the command. Not exactly rule book procedure, but a hell of a lot of fun.

On that first flight Colonel Juhn admitted he hadn't flown a DC-4 and told me to take her up, and after the tests took over so he could get the feel of the bird. He wanted to try a short landing but couldn't be comfortable with it and asked how to do it. I explained that the bird had very efficient flaps and was close to the ground, so you had a lot of ground effect to make you float.

"That makes sense," he said. "Can you land this short?" It had been a while since South America, but I said I'd try. We changed seats and took off. I climbed to 2000 feet and went into the downwind leg. He looked at me. "Downwind leg at 2000?" I just nodded, turned short, and dropped the nose. This time he looked harder and said "I hope you know what you're doing!" I said, "Gear down." He said, "*Here?*" I nodded again and fairly high I turned into base leg, told him to put the engines at 1700 and dropped the nose and called for full flaps. We practically dove for a point about 500 yards before the runway and when we were almost down I eased her back as we caught the ground effect. About 100 feet after clearing the end I touched down and we stopped without brakes halfway down the runway.

The colonel never got over that short landing and as long as he was posted at Alverca we had long conversations about flying. He was most interested in the power setting, which I explained this way: On the DC-4 the setting was to keep the engines warm, yet without drag or power, we came in high, our nose well down, airspeed maintained at about 100 mph until the last.

Like compliments, fun and fringe benefits are the kind of thing that keep you happy in a job. I worked for the military at OGMA for eleven years, from 1962 to 1973.

By 1969 the Portuguese operation was well known among U.S. military aviation people in Europe. Experiencing labor problems with their Italian contractor in Naples, the U.S. Navy came to call on us with a drop-in maintenance contract in hand. They were looking for another repair base for damaged and high-time aircraft from Sixth Fleet carriers in the Mediterranean.

The Navy explained the importance of getting birds back on board as soon as possible. I explained the importance of their supplying parts so we could do that. They agreed and sent in a C-130 well stocked with parts and personnel. That contract led to our working with a variety of Navy birds. For me, it was a valuable opportunity to continue the transition to jet engines under the enthusiastic tutelage of a fine Navy chief named Max Lansford. While with Ethiopian Airlines I had studied installations for jet engine overhaul at the new airport in Addis, but this was hands-on work where Max put me into the pit for run-ups. It may be possible to teach a crusty old ramp rat new tricks, after all!

Our first job for the Navy was to repair an F-4 that had sustained serious fire structural damage on the fuselage and aft wing structure. We got it out five days ahead of schedule. Next the Navy sent us a KA-3 with nose section damage due to a cold-shot off the carrier deck, too badly damaged to fly. They brought it on a carrier to Lisbon, where we put it on a big floating crane and ferried it up the Tejo River (which begins as the Tagus in Spain) to the airport. This, too, was an urgent repair job, as the KA-3 was a refueling bird that needed to get back into service. We had to manufacture new parts for it and Max never left the job except to grab occasional sleep in the office. That aircraft also went out ahead of schedule. Next, we repaired a badly damaged A-7 to the disbelief of the Navy's maintenance people at Cherry Point in North Carolina. An inspection team, which they sent to be sure it had been done correctly, was unable to find the repairs and had to ask us to point them out, which we did with great satisfaction.

Aircraft and maintenance techniques had advanced far beyond anything we conceived of back in the thirties, but I never lost the aversion to waste I had learned from Franklin Rose in Oakland forty years earlier. Thanks not only to Max but the support of U.S. Navy Commander Ed Melvin, then responsible for the maintenance and repair of Sixth Fleet aircraft and today one of my closest friends, we saved birds that otherwise would have been consigned to scrap. A Grumman E-2, an A-7, some SB-2Cs, Super DC-3s, and six P-3s were returned to service from OGMA because we applied old-fashioned American ingenuity. Navy inspectors went back to the States with reports that OGMA was performing repairs faster and cheaper, and with less equipment, than any domestic or foreign repair base in use by the U.S. Navy.

As time went by, Polly and I felt that at last we had left the Ethiopian experience behind. Then one day we walked into a favorite Lisbon restaurant and were astonished to be confronted by an Ethiopian Airlines man who had worked in my shop in Addis Ababa. Glad to see him, I asked what he was doing in Portugal. Before he could answer, though, I realized he had been sent to look for me.

"Well, you have found me. What are you going to do about it?" I asked him.

"No, I have not found you, Mr. Kennedy. You were very good to me when I worked for you. I'm going back to Addis and tell them I was unsuccessful in locating you." I thanked him, he left the restaurant, and that was the last I ever heard from Haile Selassie's minions.

Our life in Portugal was pleasant and fulfilling. We had a nice apartment near downtown Lisbon, an easy commute to Alverca, and Polly constantly found new fields of interest in a fascinating and historic capital. Always the student, she expertly put together a valuable stamp collection and, having done that, set about acquiring the expertise to accumulate an even more valuable collection of gold coins, earning the rare respect of Lisbon dealers. She also was foresighted enough to talk me into buying a little farm in north central Portugal, approximately eighty kilometers west of the Spanish border, which is 28 kilometers west of the town of Guarda. It was a good partnership. I thoroughly enjoyed the aviation work that made it possible for her to secure our future, a skill at which she was vastly more adept than I am.

But it was not to last. In the early seventies, Polly's mental condition, which had appeared to stablize for several years, suddenly deteriorated. I could only watch as she became virtually unmanagable. The Portuguese doctors finally diagnosed the acute schizophrenia as incurable. In October of 1972 a sudden, terribly violent crisis occurred that might have cost my life if a friend had not been there to intervene. This time I was forced to move her to a Lisbon hospital, where she was to remain until her death on July 1, 1978.

Losing Polly that way devastated me. She had been at my side for forty wonderful years, supporting and sharing a lifetime of travel and experiences we couldn't have dreamed possible and endearing herself to everyone we met, wherever we went. Different as we were, we had seldom even argued, so it was particularly difficult when my visits to her produced such raging outbursts that finally the doctors told me not to come anymore.

I didn't handle it well. I drank, and brooded. Distraught, I got rid of the Mercedes because it reminded me of her, destroyed nearly every token of our life together, including a large box of invaluable photographs, and looked for solace in ways totally alien to our relationship.

I wallowed in black despair far too long. But I was very fortunate. Miraculously, another woman almost literally appeared at my door. Her warm Portuguese mothering instinct helped me sort things out. Lidia is totally unlike Polly, which is to say only that these two women introduced entirely different but happy dimensions to my life. Stable and nurturing, a child of the earth, it was Lidia who insisted on visiting and caring for Polly. Lidia was the one person who had a calming effect on a once brilliant, now deeply disturbed woman.

During this turbulent time in my personal affairs, it did not help that I was forced into retirement in 1973 at the age of sixty, not "Civil Service wise" enough to forestall a bureaucratic snafu that the U. S. Air Force learned of too late to halt. Gradually putting the pieces of my life back together after being "riffed" from the job, I freelanced as an aviation consultant for awhile. Then a Portuguese friend who owned a PVC company hired me to get maintenance in order and the machines back into service at the factory. An entrepreneur of considerable experience, in 1974 he sent me to Luanda in Angola to investigate possibilities for the aviation industry there and to try to sell some airplanes.

It was a fascinating, if unsuccessful operation, as this was just after the revolution in Portugal, and the Angolans were fighting among themselves for control of the country once it was freed from colonial status. I managed to convince the diamond company Dimagg that they were inefficiently using two small turbo-prop English birds for their work and that a C-130 would be vastly more useful to them in transporting equipment and personnel. They did a study and agreed that one flight a day with a C-130 would move more than a week's operation with the two small kites.

I located an L-100 that Alaska Airlines wanted to sell and Dimagg gave me a check for $250,000 to hold the bird for them. But when the American consul called me to report that the State Department would not allow that bird in Angola, I had to return the check.

The fighting was getting really dangerous around our hotel, so on October 27, fifteen days before Angolan independence was declared, we got the last plane out of Luanda. It was half full of passengers and half full of freight, but it was not going back to Europe, much to the advantage of travel-minded passengers. With machine guns rattling all over the airport, the 707 took off for Rio de Janeiro—then Lima, Los Angeles, New York, Paris, and finally Lisbon. On one phenomenally cheap ticket, thanks to Angolan deflation, I was able to stop off in North Hollywood for a month to see old friends and family, and polish off the trip with ten days in Paris.

After that misadventure I was glad to return to Civil Service in the U.S. when my friend Ed Melvin, transferred to Long Beach, California, to head the NAVPRO (Naval Plant Representative) office at the Douglas Aircraft Company, asked me to help solve some production and ground maintenance equipment problems on the KC-10 refueling aircraft.

While I was in Southern California word arrived that Polly had died. Two weeks later, Lidia and I were married in Los Angeles, attended by Ed Melvin, Virginia Donohugh, the Eddie Coopers, my cousin Mildred Blake, who acted as Lidia's godmother, and her husband, Bob. Life in Southern California was pleasant and comparatively luxurious for a Portuguese country girl, but Lidia was homesick. So we returned to our farm on the outskirts of the village of Celorico da Beira.

I am convinced that anyone who has spent a lifetime with airplanes never really wants to retire from aviation, and I've been more fortunate than I probably deserve. Good old A&P license #12001 is alive and kicking. At the age of seventy-eight I'm back at work, and it's good to be around airplanes again.

My employer? None other than my old friend Ed Melvin, now

*Ed Melvin and Art Kennedy in Alverca, Portugal, 1991.*

retired from the Navy but still active in the airplane business. His company, Alverca Aerotek International, obtained the Portuguese franchise to manufacture the little American-made single engine two-seater Kitfox, an aircraft amazingly reminiscent of the thirties. It flies like the thirties, too. You can even crop-dust with it; stall speed is thirty-five miles an hour and on floats it will take off from a meadow pond practically straight up. I can sit in the right-hand seat, close my eyes, and feel exactly like a sixteen-year-old kid again, floating over Oakland with Frank Rose yelling instructions at me. Alverca Aerotek International also has some aircraft maintenance contracts with OGMA, so I'm busier than I've ever been.

Fortunately, Lidia and I had kept her small apartment in Lisbon, where I live while working, and she commutes by train to the farm to keep an eye on the our Sierra sheepdog, two promiscuous cats, the vineyards from which come the wonderful red wine we drink, our potato crop, and the water system that originates in the Roman-built springs high up on the mountain above our 200-year-old house.

I guess life comes full circle for the lucky ones. I love being back in aviation, but look forward to returning to the rural countryside in this land of warm and happy people who are fine, caring friends. In the meantime, when anyone shows up for some good hangar flying, the memories virtually tumble over one another as though they had been created only yesterday.

Looking back at more than half a century in this business, I know that my career in aviation has been blessed with remarkable experiences and remarkable people. I may never outlive my reputation as a bullshit artist, but I have been as honest in telling this life story as a good memory permits. My greatest hope is that I have made, and can continue to make, some contribution to the aviation industry. I owe it that, because aviation is still giving this old ramp rat one hell of a great life!

# Index